POWER TRIP

U.S. UNILATERALISM
AND GLOBAL STRATEGY
AFTER SEPTEMBER 11

POWER TRIP
U.S. UNILATERALISM
AND GLOBAL STRATEGY
AFTER SEPTEMBER 11

EDITED BY
JOHN FEFFER

SEVEN STORIES PRESS

NEW YORK • LONDON • TORONTO • MELBOURNE

Seven Stories Press
140 Watts Street
New York, NY 10013
www.sevenstories.com

In Canada: Hushion House, 36 Northline Road, Toronto, Ontario M4B 3E2

In the U.K.: Turnaround Publisher Services Ltd., Unit 3, Olympia Trading Estate, Coburg Road, Wood Green, London N22 6TZ

In Australia: Palgrave Macmillan, 627 Chapel Street, South Yarra, VIC 3141

LIBRARY OF CONGRESS CATALOGING-IN-PUBLICATION DATA

Power trip : U.S. unilateralism and global strategy after September 11 / edited by John Feffer.– A Seven Stories Press 1st ed.
    p. cm.
Includes bibliographical references (p.   ).
ISBN 1-58322-579-X (pbk.)
1. United States—Foreign relations—2001– 2. Unilateral acts (International law) I. Feffer, John.
E895 .P68 2003
327.73—dc21   2003009600

Printed in Canada.

9 8 7 6 5 4 3 2 1

Contents

ACKNOWLEDGMENTS 7

PREFACE by Barbara Ehrenreich 9

INTRODUCTION by John Feffer 14

CHAPTER ONE
How Things Have Changed by Tom Barry 28

CHAPTER TWO
The People by Tom Barry and Jim Lobe 39

CHAPTER THREE
The Policies 50
  Resources by Michael T. Klare 50
  Military by William D. Hartung 60
  International Law by Jules Lobel
    and Michael Ratner 74
  Foreign Economic Policy by Mark Weisbrot 85
  Intelligence by Mel Goodman 96
  Culture by Noy Thrupkaew 106

CHAPTER FOUR
The Archipelago of "Evil" 117
  Central Asia by Ahmed Rashid 117
  Middle East by Stephen Zunes 128
  Africa by Martha Honey 138
  Latin America by Coletta Youngers 150
  Asia by John Gershman 161

CHAPTER FIVE
The Response by John Feffer. 173

CHAPTER SIX
How Things Should Change
by Miriam Pemberton and John Feffer 184

AFTERWORD by Susan F. Hirsch 195

APPENDIX A
U.S. List of Foreign Terrorist Organizations 202

APPENDIX B
The Project for the New American Century 205

APPENDIX C
Americans for Victory Over Terrorism 210

APPENDIX D
Going It Alone 211

RESOURCES 215

NOTES 227

ABOUT THE CONTRIBUTORS 250

SPONSORING ORGANIZATIONS 252

Acknowledgments

LIKE OTHER BOOKS, the credits for *Power Trip* extend far beyond the writers and editors, including virtually the entire staff of Foreign Policy In Focus (FPIF) at its two sponsoring organizations: Institute for Policy Studies (IPS) and the Interhemispheric Resource Center (IRC). However, we would like first to acknowledge that this book, like FPIF itself, is in many ways a product of a long intellectual and activist tradition in the United States that has advocated a more responsible and constructive use of U.S. power in international affairs. This book and its contributors are themselves the product of many decades of advocacy campaigns for human rights, demilitarization, international cooperation, the international rule of law, and other progressive values. We acknowledge our moral and intellectual debt to this long, proud history of progressive advocacy and analysis.

Power Trip is the end result of a determination by the FPIF Advisory Committee that FPIF's "think tank without walls" should respond to the dangerous new directions of the Bush foreign policy with a comprehensive critique of how the U.S. is abusing its position of supremacy in the post-9/11 era. John Feffer, as editor, took this conviction and converted it into a book bringing together some of the best analysts associated with Foreign Policy In Focus. His professionalism, wordsmithing, management, and his own writing contribution made the book possible, and we thank him profusely.

We want also to express our appreciation to the writers who took time from their busy schedules to present such expert, insightful analysis of the exercise of U.S. military, economic, cultural, and diplomatic power. But this book is about more than a collection of good writing and perspicacious analysis. The most important acknowledgment will come from those who read this book. By taking the analysis offered in these pages by the FPIF analysts and integrating it in our own educational, organizing, and political involvement, we will at the same time acknowledge the value of these expert contributions and the enduring wisdom of progressive principles.

At the Institute for Policy Studies, key staff members and interns who contributed with research and managing the many details involved in the creation of a book include Erik Leaver, Shannon Roe, Irmak Ince, Michelle Mendez, and Julliette Neihuss. We also want to thank John Cavanagh, IPS executive director, for his strong support for Foreign Policy In Focus.

At the Interhemispheric Resource Center, staff members involved in research assistance include Siri Khalsa, Nancy Stockdale, and IRC Executive Director Debra Preusch.

Special thanks goes to Greg Ruggiero, our editor at Seven Stories Press, for his patience and his shared conviction in the importance of such a book project about the new power trip launched by the Bush administration. Finally, we gratefully acknowledge the foundations including John D. and Catherine T. MacArthur Foundation and the Ford Foundation for their continuing support of Foreign Policy In Focus as well as special dedicated support for this book project from the American Friends Service Committee and Friends Committee on National Legislation.

Martha Honey and Tom Barry

Preface

by Barbara Ehrenreich

ON THE MORNING of September 11, 2001, I turned on the TV in my hotel room to catch the latest news about the missing congressional intern, Chandra Levy. Maybe that's not what I wanted to see, but it's all I was likely to see on CNN, which had devoted the summer almost exclusively to the case. We'd had O.J. Simpson, we'd had Tonya Harding and Monica Lewinsky, and now the cable news channels were, as we liked to say that summer, "all Chandra, all the time." So the images of planes crashing into buildings, followed by buildings crashing to the earth, did not, at first, compute. If anyone had a motive, I figured in my post-traumatic stupor, it had to be Levy's boss and erstwhile lover, Gary Condit.

The events of that morning went far beyond anything that could be handled by the usual cliché of a "wake-up call." We Americans had been lazy, willfully ignorant, and self-involved to the point of solipsism. If there was an outside world, we didn't want to know about it, unless the death of a beautiful princess was involved. And now here it was: palpable, in-your-face evidence of the existence of people unlike ourselves, people who were in fact murderously hostile to us and clever enough to eclipse even Chandra Levy.

We had been following, I now realized, the plotline of innumerable horror films, in which the thoughtless teenagers party hard in some ramshackle, out-of-the-way site until one of the group shows up dead and hideously mutilated. At this point they realize that they are not alone, that someone is out there, some incomprehensible Other who wants them dead. But with the beer flowing and the hormones surging, they have no way of organizing against the threat.

Many Americans responded, in those first few months after the attack, in generous and intelligent ways. They sent aid to the victims' families; they bought up books on Islam and learned to distinguish between Arabs and Muslims, moderates and fundamentalists, Sufis and Wahhabists. In some communities, good-hearted people reached out to the Arab-Americans, Sikhs, and Hindus who were suddenly facing vengeful harassment from the incorrigibly ignorant. Churches shared Ramadan feasts with mosques; students assembled for teach-ins. We were playing a desperate game of catch-up, trying to comprehend a whole world—that of Islam—we'd dismissed as too musty and backward to bother with.

But now that we were awake, we also needed to respond—a point that the brave antiwar demonstrators who briefly flourished in the fall of 2001 did not always seem to grasp. When someone declares "death to Americans"—babies and old people alike, not to mention Jews, Israelis, and possibly Christians—you've got an enemy, like it or not. I for one did not want to earn my frequent-flyer miles wrestling with sui-cide-killers. With great reluctance and foreboding, I had to agree with the Bush administration that America needed to launch a "war on terror" or at least a determined effort to apprehend the terrorists.

How to go about it, though? Terrorists, by definition, lack the obvious targets, like capital cities, government buildings, and uniformed armies. They are warriors without a state or, in this case, even a clear-cut geographical point of concentration. As it soon emerged, the presumptive comrades of the

September 11 suicide-bombers were scattered around the globe—in Saudi Arabia, Egypt, Sudan, Somalia, Germany, France, Indonesia, England, Pakistan, and the Philippines. An enormous amount of intelligence, in every sense of the word, would be required to flush them out: cells would have to be infiltrated, prospective defectors courted, investigations launched all over the world. Plus, of course, we'd have to try to understand the roots of their bitterness and the conditions—of both poverty and thwarted middle-class ambitions—that nourished them. We would have to do this if we wanted a real "war on terror"—not a conventional war but a systematic approach to addressing a difficult and dangerous problem, like the "war on poverty" was supposed to be.

What we got is something very different. First there was the war against Afghanistan, which at least had the advantage of being a far more familiar type of military target than a diffuse international network of terrorists. No one can mourn the fiendish Taliban regime, which American and British bombs quickly displaced, but other than that, it is hard to know, a year later, what exactly the war accomplished. Are the leaders of al-Qaeda dead or merely scattered? Have their far-flung cells been rendered headless and impotent, or were they decentralized enough to carry on independently? If the goal was to crush terrorism, there is no way of knowing whether this war succeeded.

As for Afghanistan, it is in little better shape today than it was before the Taliban's fall, with hunger rampant, war lords riding high in the countryside, and most women still too fearful to emerge from their burkas. An unknown number of civilians—somewhere between five hundred and three thousand—managed to get in the way of our bombs and the bullets, winning us the lasting enmity of their survivors. Maybe all we won was the fleeting satisfaction of countering violence with violence, however misdirected—like those traditional societies in New Guinea in which even deaths by disease were "avenged" by going to war against a neighboring village.

But at least, in Afghanistan, our leaders were still ostensibly waging a war on terrorism. For reasons unclear to the rest of the world—attention deficit disorder or possibly early-stage Alzheimer's—that project is now being dropped. Al-Qaeda may still be festering on three or four continents, preparing to dispatch thousands more Americans by plane-bombs or poison. But we are now at war with, of all places, Iraq.

Why not Germany, where some of the pre–September 11 plotting took place, or Saudi Arabia, which supplied fifteen of the nineteen perpetrators? Or, if the idea is to topple headstrong, potentially roguish leaders who have the means of mass destruction at their fingertips, why not Pakistan, North Korea, India, or Sharon's belligerent Israel? There are no known connections between Saddam Hussein and Osama bin Laden, aside from a history of mutual dislike, and no reason to start a new war when the old one is nowhere near finished. One can't help suspect that our leaders sense they haven't gotten far in the war against terrorism and are eager to change the subject.

Whatever motivates current U.S. foreign policy—oil, domestic politics, or the Oedipal rage of a lackluster son—it isn't likely to make us any safer. The war in Afghanistan, combined with Bush's meek stance toward Sharon, has already convinced Muslims throughout the world that their lives have no value to America's leaders. The invasion of Iraq and the attendant "collateral damage" will harden the impression that the United States is pursuing its own kind of jihad—against the Islamic world. Inevitably, a generation of young Muslims in Riyadh or Cairo or Hamburg will seek martyrdom by taking some of us out.

So here we are, caught inside the horror film we know so well from the screen. September 11 awakened us briefly from our fantasies of sex and murder and weight loss to the existence of an implacably hostile Other. But like the partying teens in the movies, the people in charge can't seem to figure out a way of responding that doesn't recklessly escalate the danger.

Introduction

by John Feffer

PRIOR TO TAKING office in January 2001, George W. Bush was largely a foreign policy cipher. His lack of international experience and overseas travel suggested a personal isolationism that might very well translate into a foreign policy disposition. Bush additionally promised to focus on domestic priorities, so if only by default the new administration was expected to maintain a measure of continuity with the mainstream of U.S. foreign policy. And indeed, in its first months the administration calmed European allies, reached out to Russia, and sought increased engagement with Mexico. Tyrants were to be tweaked, but military campaigns to displace them were not initially in the offing. Although the new foreign policy team was unapologetic about U.S. hegemony, they appeared to aim for a prudent preeminence.[1]

At the same time, Bush appeared to be groping around for a foreign policy that was neither isolationist nor multilateral. He therefore decisively repudiated his predecessor's attempts to secure a rapprochement with North Korea and, in a sop to the anti-China lobby, strengthened security relations with Taiwan. There were also promises to enhance the military and rescue U.S. sovereignty from the clutches of international institutions. Bush signaled the end of the Anti-Ballistic Missile Treaty, pulled out of the Kyoto protocol on global warming, indicated he would reverse what was already tepid U.S. support for the International Criminal Court, and served notice that the United States was perfectly comfortable standing outside of international consensus.

Two camps clearly competed for Bush's ear on foreign policy: hard-liners such as Secretary of Defense Donald Rumsfeld, his deputy Paul Wolfowitz, and Vice President Dick Cheney, and realists in the classic mold such as Secretary of State Colin Powell. Powell stood for continuity with the major trends in post–Cold War foreign policy: a commitment to U.S. hegemony but by less confrontational means, with the support of allies, and according to a traditional balance-of-power calculus. The hard-liners, however, had a very clear agenda for transforming U.S. foreign policy along the lines of the Reagan revolution of the 1980s. This time, though, the Soviet Union was gone, and the United States had unparalleled power. The hard-liners urged Bush to cut loose the United States from its moorings in the international system. In such a scenario, a newly confident United States intoxicated with its own military, economic, and political preeminence would set out to remake the world in its own image, targeting adversaries, ignoring allies, and acting with all the arrogance of a country that believes itself above criticism, a country in short that is on a power trip.

To effect this transformation, the hard-liners were up against more significant obstacles than simply Colin Powell. At home, the Bush administration faced a public reluctant to accept American casualties in extended wars, domestic criticism of high defense spending and skewed budget priorities, fears of the impact of free trade on U.S. jobs and the global environment, and even questions about the very legitimacy of the political process that brought George Bush into the White House with a minority of the popular vote and a razor-thin margin of victory in Florida. After Jim Jeffords of Vermont defected to the independent camp in May 2001, the Republicans lost their majority in the Senate and Bush's maneuvering room was consequently narrowed. Abroad, the hard-liners had to contend with considerable resistance to

the United States after September 11, has taken a stunning U-turn against the Bush administration and its policies.

This anti-Americanism has only increased now that the war in Afghanistan has been replaced in the headlines by the war in Iraq that began in March 2003. Unlike Gulf War I, few countries have joined the Anglo-U.S. campaign to oust Saddam Hussein. By forsaking a multilateral approach to addressing Iraq's actual or potential weapons of mass destruction, the Bush administration has managed to alienate key European allies, most Arab countries, large swaths of the developing world, and even North American neighbors Canada and Mexico. The big stick the U.S. deployed after September 11 with devastating consequences in Afghanistan and Iraq has stirred up a global hornet's nest.

A year and a half after September 11, the Bush administration has a clearly established foreign policy doctrine—summarized in a thirty-one-page position paper;[5] embraced by a political party that has regained control of both houses of Congress; and implemented by U.S. soldiers, diplomats, and trade representatives throughout the world. The war on terrorism, like the war on Communism before it, serves as an organizing principle, combining with a zeal for military preeminence and a drive to secure more foreign oil to form a threefold path to global dominance. While the Bush administration did not conceal its preference for military solutions to the Gordian knots of international relations prior to September 11, the new military policy recognizes few limits, emphasizes rollback over containment, and breaks taboos on the role of preemptive strikes and the use of nuclear weapons. This new military doctrine fits tongue-and-groove with a rigid unilateralism that threatens to unravel the international system of institutions and legal precedents built up over fifty years. Despite a marked preference for "hard" over "soft" power, the Bush administration has nevertheless continued to try to win the "hearts and minds" of people at home and abroad through a cultural campaign and to continue to secure overseas markets for U.S. business through both targeted subsidies and the application of neoliberalism and free-trade nostrums. In the following chapters, contributors will explore in more detail these facets of the new Bush doctrine.

THE ARCHIPELAGO OF EVIL

When George Bush announced that Iran, Iraq, and North Korea belonged to an "axis of evil" in his State of the Union speech in January 2002, he was being both illogical and entirely consistent.

For the better part of the 1990s, the United States maintained a shortlist of "rogue nations"—briefly euphemized as "states of concern" by the Clinton administration—that consisted of seven states officially designated as exporters of terrorism: Iran, Iraq, North Korea, Sudan, Syria, Libya, and Cuba. Afghanistan would have been on the list if the United States had recognized the Taliban's rule as legitimate. By 2002, the list had shrunk for obvious reasons: the Taliban was gone; Syria, Sudan, and Libya had quietly offered assistance in the war on terrorism; and Cuba was simply too weak to pose any credible threat. Other countries that might qualify as exporters of terrorism, such as Pakistan or India, have been too busy being U.S. allies to moonlight as axis members. Saudi Arabia and Egypt, the home countries for the September 11 hijackers, have been receiving billions of dollars in U.S. military hardware for decades. Traditional adversaries Russia and China, fighting their own "terrorists" in Chechnya and Xinjiang, signed up early for the global war on terrorism. Iran, Iraq, and the conveniently non-Islamic North Korea (to anticipate the objections of the Muslim world) were the last candidates left.

Plot the coordinates of Operation Enduring Freedom in Afghanistan and the axis of evil, and a much older pattern begins to emerge. The Bush administration is battling for control of the holy grail of geopolitics: the Eurasian heartland. Numerous empires have sought control of the territory that stretches from the plains of Europe to the populous lands of Asia. In the early twentieth century, British military strategist Halford Mackinder raised the control of this area to the status of a geopolitical law; during World War II, American Nicholas Spykman modified Mackinder's theories to emphasize naval control of the bordering regions of Eurasia.[6] Afghanistan, Iran, Iraq, and North Korea are thus gateways to controlling the heartland. Instead of a cold war between east and west, George Bush has resurrected a much older confrontation, a great game among the remaining great powers for control of Eurasia and its tremendous natural resources.[7]

Yet the Bush formulation is also illogical. There is no axis of evil, for there is no axis. An axis implies a group of states working together toward a particular goal. Iran and Iraq fought one of the bloodiest wars of the Cold War period, and today regard each other with animosity and wariness. For the purposes of acquiring hard currency or high technology, North Korea will trade with one or the other, but North Korea's ideological mix of Communism and Confucianism contrasts sharply with Iran's fundamentalism and Iraq's petrofascism. However these three countries are identified—rogues, states of concern, anti-American, or just plain paranoid—they form not an axis but an archipelago: separate islands of resistance to the United States. The other countries and non-state actors that might find themselves in this archipelago are similarly unrelated: Osama bin Laden can't abide Saddam Hussein, the Colombian guerrillas have no relationship with Iran, Islamic fundamentalists in

Central Asia do not look further east to North Korea for guidance.

U.S. policy toward the "axis" might on the surface seem inconsistent. Washington has opted for a military solution in Iraq but has called for a diplomatic resolution of the crisis that re-erupted in December 2002 involving North Korea's nuclear program. At a deeper level, however, the Bush administration wants regime change in both countries and believes fundamentally that negotiations with "evil" countries are not feasible.

In the essays in this section, contributors will demonstrate that the "war on terrorism" has much larger global goals than targeting Iran, Iraq, and North Korea. The Eurasian heartland lies at the center of U.S. policy, but the Bush administration has truly global aspirations. In Asia, the Middle East, Latin America, and Africa, the administration has switched from containing adversarial regimes to replacing them. The result, namely the weakening of moderate forces and the hardening of extremism, is proving so far to be the exact opposite of what the administration says it wants.

HOW THINGS HAVEN'T CHANGED

No administration, however radical its intentions or substantial its political capital, can escape history. While indeed heralding a sea change in U.S. foreign policy, the Bush administration's policies and pronouncements nevertheless owe a great deal to the past.

During the Cold War, the isolationist and internationalist tendencies in U.S. policy coalesced into a liberal-conservative consensus on countering Communism on the battlefield and in the marketplace. Although liberal internationalists managed to win approval for U.S. participation in a new global political and economic architecture (the

UN, World Bank), the face-off with the Soviet Union dictated that multilateralism be subordinated to the larger anti-Communist struggle. Key institutions such as the Alliance for Progress, NATO, and the European Community were designed to contain Soviet influence. The national security state, the military-industrial complex, a succession of military interventions—these did not arise because one political party imposed its agenda on the country. Democrats and Republicans joined hands in this enterprise until U.S. defeat in the Vietnam War drove a wedge into this consensus.

After Jimmy Carter briefly flirted with a more moral foreign policy, the Reagan administration irrevocably altered the way the United States interacted with the world. The Reagan years represented a surge in unilateralism, as the United States flouted international law, undermined treaties, and consistently stood outside of consensus at the UN.[8] Not content to contain the rival superpower and clearly opposed to detente, the Reagan team sought to roll back Communism at the very borders of the Soviet Union, through support of the mujahedin in Afghanistan and covert funding of the opposition in Poland. The military budget ballooned; interventions in the Third World continued directly or through proxies. Many of the hard-liners in the current Bush team cut their teeth in the Reagan years, as their preferences for unilateralism and militarism would indicate.

After the Cold War, the search began for a new national interest that could substitute for containing or rolling back Communism. The Pentagon, its very raison d'etre at question, was perhaps quickest off the mark. It defined the national interest as a series of largely asymmetric threats that required countering: competitors such as China that might one day confront the United States head on, "rogue states" such as Iran and Iraq that retained sufficient military power to challenge U.S interests in key regions, proliferators of missile technology such as North Korea, and non-state actors such as terrorists and narco-traffickers (and the states that supported them). Missile defense, once the domain of the lunatic fringe, returned in the 1990s as a high-tech answer to these threats. The United States pushed for the expansion of NATO over the objections of Russia. Despite the disappearance of the Soviet threat, levels of defense spending remained the same on average as during the Cold War. Although the military explored new capabilities, from peacekeeping to environmental cleanup, the United States continued to rely heavily on the language of militarism to interact with other countries.

The 1990s were supposed to be a time when the United States reconfigured its role in the world. Bush Sr. proclaimed a "new world order" that, in Panama and the Persian Gulf, looked a great deal like the old world order, minus the Soviet military. Bill Clinton came into office promoting an "assertive multilateralism." But then, ten months into his term, Clinton watched his very own new world order self-destruct on the streets of Mogadishu when what began as a humanitarian operation to feed starving Somalis ended in a firefight that left eighteen Americans dead. Clinton pulled the United States out of Somalia and out of the more deliberate engagement with the world that he originally envisioned.

"Crossing the Mogadishu line," an updated version of the "Vietnam complex," would be the cautionary brake on U.S. global engagement in the 1990s. As Walter Russell Mead explains, "The very plenitude of occasions for such intervention was the most powerful argument against humanitarian interventions; Americans could see no limit to the calls on their purse or their troops if Wilsonian interventionism became the cornerstone of American policy."[9] Pentagon officials became obsessed with "exit strategy" (how to get out) and "mission creep" (a campaign that stretches to embrace new tasks and lasts longer than mandated).

This concern for getting caught in a Vietnam War–like quagmire prevented the United States from intervening to stop genocide in Rwanda, to preserve "safe havens" in Bosnia, and, after a single anti-American demonstrator in Haiti screamed "we are going to turn this into another Somalia" at a U.S.-led boatload of UN troops, to bring a peaceful resolution more quickly to the standoff between a military junta and the popular movements in Haiti.[10] Efforts to end the war in Yugoslavia and safeguard the independence of East Timor were delegated where possible to others, the Croatian army in the first case and Australian peacekeepers in the second. When the United States did initiate a military campaign—the air war against Serbia in 1999—it had already internalized the Mogadishu mantra of "leave no man behind" to such a degree that this became the first military engagement in modern history with no casualties for the victors.

The "international interest" played only a minor supporting role in this reconfiguring of the "national interest." There were voices in the Clinton administrations that supported authentic multilateralism and honest humanitarianism, that saw the United States in partnership with rather than lording over the rest of the world. But as the 1990s progressed, the United States consistently manipulated international institutions for its own ends, piling up conditions on when, where, and how it would work with others. Despite vaunted claims of a new age of multilateralism, "the years of the Clinton presidency have seen the United States drift toward unilateralism and the undermining of the international system," former State Department official Wayne Smith concluded in 1999.[11] Another former government official, Charles William Maynes, concurred one year later: "It is ironic that the tenure of Madeleine Albright, the first secretary of State to serve as the permanent U.S. representative to the United Nations, may well mark the lowest point in Washington approach toward multilateralism since World War II."[12]

During the Clinton era, a Congress controlled by Republicans after the 1994 elections could certainly take credit for much of this unilateralism after its rejection of key treaties involving the environment, biosafety, and nuclear tests and because of its persistence in holding back funds from the UN. But the Clinton administration conceded these battles without much struggle.[13] The administration also rejected the landmines treaty because of Pentagon opposition, signed the treaty establishing the International Criminal Court but refused to recommend ratification, stretched the Anti-Ballistic Missile Treaty to near breaking point, maneuvered unilaterally to oust UN General Secretary Boutros Boutros-Ghali after a single term, undertook military actions in Iraq and Kosovo without UN approval, relied on NATO for military actions to provide a semblance of multilateralism, and launched counterterrorism strikes in Afghanistan and Sudan without building a case or a coalition.[14]

Joseph Nye argues that while the U.S. acts unilaterally in the military realm, the economic sphere should be more accurately described as multipolar.[15] This greater dispersion of economic power, with Japan and the European Union both substantial players, has not prevented the United States from attempting to preserve and extend its economic hegemony. Whether this was through free trade mechanisms or the maintenance of domestic subsidies (agriculture, defense, energy, steel) has depended on circumstance, not ideology. The United States played hardball in trade negotiations in order to protect U.S. advantages, not build a fair or neutral international trade system.[16]

much of that constituency had been attracted to right-wing gadfly Patrick Buchanan, who shared its "traditional values" but who also strongly opposed the Gulf War and has long deplored the more imperial, neoconservative influence in the Republican Party. Two other groups, the Center for Security Policy and Empower America, played a similar role with respect to forging a new coalition behind the goal of U.S. military and cultural supremacy.

Whatever the validity of U.S. military supremacy theory as a legitimate or effective defense posture, the ideology has immediate rewards for U.S. weapons manufacturers. This nexus of military strategists and the military industry is epitomized by the right-wing Center for Security Policy, with its close connections to both military contractors and the Pentagon.[49] The Center's director, Frank Gaffney, one of the original signatories of the PNAC statement in 1997, rejoiced that his group's "peace through strength" principles have once again found a place in U.S. government. Like the Reagan years, when many of the center's current associates directed U.S. military policy, the present administration includes a large number of members of the Center's National Security Advisory Council. An early member of the Center's board, Dick Cheney, is now vice president, and Defense Secretary Donald Rumsfeld was a recipient of the Center's Keeper of the Flame award.

Since the 1970s, neoconservatives had been exploring the global-local links of the "culture war." In the view of the Christian Right, core American values were under attack by a liberal cultural elite that espoused secular humanism and ethical relativism. For neoconservatives, however, the culture war was an international one that threatened the entire Judeo-Christian culture. One of the earliest groups taking this position was the Ethics and Public Policy Center, which was established in 1976 "to clarify and reinforce the bond between Judeo-Christian moral tradition and the public policy debate over domestic and foreign policy issues."[50] The Ethics and Public Policy Center, where Elliott Abrams was an associate in the 1990s before he joined the Bush administration, explored the common moral ground (and common concerns) that Jewish and Catholic conservatives shared with the Christian Right. Long a theme in American politics, the idea of America's cultural supremacy and the need to defend it against mounting international attack had by the late 1990s become a powerful theme in the U.S. political debate. Neoconservative historian Samuel Huntington provided theoretical cover for this paranoid sense of cultural supremacy in his influential *The Clash of Civilizations and the Remaking of World Order.*[51]

Former "drug czar" and education secretary William J. Bennett, another signatory of the PNAC 1997 statement, has had the most success in making the local-global links in the culture war. Together with Jack Kemp, Bennett in 1999 founded Empower America, a right-wing policy group that argues for domestic and foreign policies informed by conservative moral values. Since September 11, Bennett's Empower America, together with subsidiary groups, has propagated the Bush administration's own message of a moral and military crusade against evil.[52] As part of its campaign to highlight the moral character of Bush's foreign policy, Empower America formed a new group called Americans for Victory Over Terrorism (AVOT) (see Appendix C). In a full-page ad in the *New York Times,* AVOT chairman Bennett warned: "The threats we face are both external and internal." Within the United States are "those who are attempting to use this opportunity [9/11] to promulgate their agenda of 'blame America first.'" In its pronouncement, AVOT identified U.S. public opinion as the key battleground in the war against America's external and internal threats. "Our goal," declared AVOT, "is to address the present threats so as to eradicate future terrorism and defeat ideologies that support it."[53] Also in the forefront of focusing attention on internal threats has been Lynne Cheney, wife of the vice president and an associate at the American Enterprise Institute, who played a lead role in founding the American Council of Trustees and Alumni (ACTA), which singled out professors deemed not sufficiently patriotic.

Under the tutelage of neoconservatives like Elliott Abrams and under the guiding hand of William Bennett, social conservatives, particularly those associated with the Christian Right, have become new internationalists.[54] Looking beyond the culture wars at home, they found new reasons for a rightist internationalism abroad. Building on the Biblical foundations for an apocalyptic confrontation in the Middle East, the Christian Right has fully supported the neoconservative agenda on U.S.-Israel relations.[55] In their literature and Internet presence, socially conservative groups such as Empower America and the Foundation for the Defense of Democracy place special emphasis on the righteousness of the military campaign against the Palestinians by the Likud Party of Israeli Prime Minister Ariel Sharon.[56] Other galvanizing issues for social conservatives are the persecution of Christians abroad, especially in Islamic countries and China, sex trafficking, and "yellow peril" threat of Communist China.

For critics, the administration's willingness to hire a handful of Reagan-era officials tainted by their illegal dealings with the Nicaraguan contras amply illustrated its moral hypocrisy, undermining any valid claim to moral clarity. These included such figures as Otto Reich, former chief of Reagan's Office of Public Diplomacy, who was appointed the State Department's chief Latin America officer despite findings that he had lied to Congress and the American public.

Other rogue officials from the Reagan administration's illegal programs to aid the contras include Elliott Abrams, John Poindexter, and John Negroponte.[57] The Bush administration, whose moral compass is officially declared to have an undeviating good-evil orientation, instead responds to a Machiavellian logic in which even the means—no matter if they violate international law and ignore human rights—justify the ends sought by an America-centric foreign policy.

BRINGING IT ALL TOGETHER

As during the Reagan administration, the right-wing think tanks have played a key role in shaping the new policy framework. Especially important has been the neoconservative American Enterprise Institute, whose most prominent member of the Bush administration is Richard Perle, the chair of Rumsfeld's Defense Planning Board.[58] Perle, a supporter of PNAC, helped establish the Center for Security Policy and the increasingly influential Jewish Institute for National Security (JINSA).[59] Over the years, AEI has been in the forefront of calling for preemptive military attacks against rogue states and has denounced as "appeasement" all efforts by Washington and its European allies to "engage" North Korea, Iran, or Iraq. The Bush administration has embraced virtually all of the policy positions that the AEI has promoted on the Middle East. Coursing through AEI policy analysis—and now through the Bush administration—is a profound belief in the inherent goodness and redemptive mission of the United States, criticism of the moral cowardice of "liberals" and "European elites," an imperative to support Israel against the "implacable hatred" of Muslims, and a conviction in the primacy of military power in an essentially Hobbesian world. Although not yet part of the official rhetoric, AEI's belief that a conflict with

China is inevitable is also one held by the hawks in the administration.

On the editorial pages of the *Weekly Standard* (published by PNAC cofounder William Kristol), the *Wall Street Journal, National Review, Commentary Magazine,* and the *Washington Times,* as well as in the nationally syndicated columns by William Safire, Michael Kelly, and Charles Krauthammer, the State Department (particularly its Near East bureau) came under steady attack.[60] But even within the State Department, the new foreign policy radicals had set up camp. Over Powell's objections, Bush appointed John Bolton, an ultra-unilateralist ideologue and former vice president of the American Enterprise Institute, as undersecretary of state for arms control and international security.

For the most part, the political right led by the neoconservatives has focused on the need for America to assert its military and diplomatic power—a focus underscored by the war on terrorism. In marked contrast to the Clinton years, the neoconservative strategists together with the hawks have sidelined the public debate about globalization. Instead of fretting over social and environmental standards in the global economy, the economic focus is on securing U.S. national interests, particularly energy resources, and thereby ensuring continued U.S. economic supremacy. A continued weakening of the U.S. economy and a rising concern of U.S. military overreach is contributing to some fracturing of the right.[61]

This small group of right-wing strategists, ideologues, and operatives in right-wing think tanks, advocacy groups, and the news media has captured U.S. foreign and military policy. The neoconservatives and hawks set the Bush administration's foreign policy agenda—an agenda of supremacy that moderate conservatives and realists came to share, for the most part, although differences remained over how this supremacy should be maintained.[62] At issue is not so much that this shift in foreign policy has been engineered by a narrow elite—given that foreign policy has traditionally been the province of conservative and liberal elites—but rather the implications of this sharp turn to the right. Clearly, a new foreign policy vision was needed to match the new global realities. But is this show of American supremacy the grand strategy that best serves U.S. national interests and security? In the end, the U.S. electorate will need to decide if they want this show of supremacy and power to go on. As Americans we will need to decide if we now feel more secure, if our economic and moral interests are better represented now, and if a foreign policy based on extending U.S. supremacy makes us proud to be Americans.

CHAPTER THREE

The Policies

RESOURCES
by Michael T. Klare

SINCE SEPTEMBER 11, the United States has been so totally involved in the war against terrorism that it is easy to conclude that fighting and winning this war is the Bush administration's sole foreign policy objective. Certainly President Bush has stated on many occasions that management of the global campaign against terror is his most important responsibility. But while an enormous effort is indeed being devoted to this campaign, antiterrorism is not the administration's only major foreign policy concern. Since taking office in early 2001, the Bush team has devoted equal attention to two other strategic priorities: the procurement of additional petroleum from foreign sources and the modernization of U.S. military capabilities. These added priorities have independent roots but have become fused with each other and with the war on terrorism to produce a unified strategic design. It is this unified design, rather than any individual objective, that now governs U.S. foreign policy.

The administration's new strategic design does not have a formal name or a written declaration of principles. But in their integrated form these three priorities are producing a decisive shift in American military behavior. Evidence of this shift can be seen in U.S. actions in several key areas of the world—Central Asia, Colombia, and the Persian Gulf.

The temporary U.S. bases established in Central Asia and the Caucasus after September 11 to support the war in Afghanistan are now being transformed into permanent facilities, giving the United States a significant military presence in the energy-rich Caspian Sea basin.

In addition to supporting the Colombian government's efforts to suppress illegal drug trafficking, the United States will now aid Bogotá in its efforts to protect vital oil pipelines against guerrilla attack.

While President Bush has argued that Saddam Hussein must be deposed in order to prevent Iraq from acquiring and using weapons of mass destruction, other U.S. officials have stressed the need to protect the flow of energy from the Persian Gulf to the United States and its allies.

These developments, and others like them in other regions of the world, are characteristic of the recent evolution of U.S. foreign policy. From now on, it will not be possible to comprehend the overall thrust of U.S. foreign policy without considering how the three strands of resource acquisition, military intervention, and counterterrorism are being integrated into a single grand strategy.

THE PURSUIT OF IMPORTED PETROLEUM

The administration's first major priority, the acquisition of additional petroleum supplies from foreign sources, was spelled out in the report of the National Energy Policy Development Group, released on May 17, 2001. Known as the Cheney report, after its principal author Vice President Dick Cheney, this document purports to provide the United States with a comprehensive blueprint for satisfying its growing energy needs over the next quarter century. This blueprint incorporates some measures for increased energy conservation, but most of the proposals in the report are aimed at expanding America's overall supply of energy.

Ever since its release, the Cheney report has been the subject of considerable controversy because it advocates oil drilling in the Arctic National Wildlife Refuge (ANWR) in Alaska and because its authors consulted regularly with officials of the now bankrupt Enron Corporation when drafting their recommendations. Unfortunately, this controversy has tended to deflect attention from the international security implications of energy policy in particular.

Only in the final chapter of the report does the true intent of the Cheney approach become apparent: America's growing demand for energy will require the import of ever-increasing supplies of foreign petroleum. According to the Cheney report, U.S. reliance on imported petroleum will rise from 52 percent of total consumption in 2001 to an estimated 66 percent in 2020.[63] Because *total* petroleum use is also rising, the United States will have to import 60 percent more oil in 2020 than it does today. In concrete terms, U.S. oil imports will have to rise from their current rate of 10.4 million barrels per day to an estimated 16.7 million barrels per day in 2020.[64] The only way to accomplish this is to persuade foreign suppliers to increase their production of oil and to sell more of their output to the United States. However, many supplying countries lack the capital to make the necessary investments in production infrastructure and/or are reluctant to allow American firms to dominate their energy sector. The Cheney report therefore calls on the White House to make the pursuit of increased oil imports "a priority of our trade and foreign policy."[65]

In particular, the report calls on the president and other top officials to pursue a two-pronged strategy to satisfy America's growing requirement for petroleum. The first goal of this strategy is to increase imports from the Persian

Gulf countries, which together possess about two-thirds of the world's known oil reserves. Recognizing that no other region can increase production as rapidly or as substantially, the report advocates a vigorous U.S. diplomatic effort to persuade the governments of Saudi Arabia and other oil-producing countries in the Gulf region to allow American firms to undertake substantial infrastructure enhancements in their countries.

The second goal of the strategy is to increase the geographic *diversity* of U.S. imports so as to reduce the economic damage that would be caused by future supply interruptions in the ever-turbulent Middle East. To promote such diversity, the report calls on the president and other top officials to work with U.S. energy firms in increasing American oil imports from the Caspian Sea basin (especially Azerbaijan and Kazakhstan), sub-Saharan Africa (especially Angola and Nigeria), and Latin America (especially Colombia, Mexico, and Venezuela).

The Cheney report does not state the obvious: namely, that virtually all of the areas identified as potential sources of increased oil supplies are chronically unstable, harbor anti-American sentiments, or both. While it is true that various elites in these countries may favor increased economic cooperation with the United States, other sectors of the population oppose such ties for nationalist, economic, or ideological reasons. Hence, U.S. efforts to obtain more petroleum from these countries are almost certain to provoke resistance, including, in some cases, terrorism and other forms of violent behavior. There is, then, an unacknowledged *security* dimension to the Cheney plan, with considerable significance for U.S. military policy. An energy policy favoring increased U.S. access to oil reserves located in chronically unstable areas such as the Persian Gulf, the Caspian Sea basin, Latin America, and sub-Saharan Africa

Top 10 Suppliers of Imported Oil to the U.S.—2002

Rank	Country	Net Imports (mbd)	% of Total Imports
1	Canada	1.94	17%
2	Saudi Arabia	1.55	13%
3	Mexico	1.53	13%
4	Venezuela	1.38	12%
5	Nigeria	0.60	5%
6	UK	0.48	4%
7	Iraq	0.44	4%
8	Norway	0.38	3%
9	Angola	0.33	3%
10	Algeria	0.27	2%
	Total	8.9	77%

Source: Energy Information Agency, U.S. Department of Energy, "Monthly Energy Review: Petroleum," January 2003. Available online at: http://www.eia.doe.gov/emeu/mer/petro.html.

will prove far more tenable if accompanied by a military strategy favoring a significant enhancement in America's capacity to project military power into these areas.

Whether or not senior political figures have consciously sought to link these two policy objectives, there is no doubt that U.S. military officials are aware of their close association. Thus, according to the Pentagon's *Quadrennial Defense Review* [QDR] *Report* of September 2001, "The United States and its allies and friends will continue to depend on the energy resources of the Middle East," and access to this vital region could be jeopardized by a variety of military threats.[66] The QDR then proceeds to describe the capabilities that the United States will need to protect its interests in the Middle East and other oil-producing areas—notably, forces designed for "power projection" (or military intervention) in distant and troubled areas.[67]

Indeed, it is this emphasis on "power projection" that forms the core of the Bush administration's military policy. Even before entering the White House, Bush spoke of the need to enhance U.S. capabilities for intervention abroad. In an important speech at the Citadel on September 23, 1999, Bush laid out his plans for the "transformation" of the American military. This entailed, among other things, the construction of a full-scale missile defense system and the acquisition of a new array of high-technology weapons. But what is most needed, Bush avowed, is the enhancement of America's capacity to rapidly transport U.S. combat forces to distant battle zones and, once deployed, to quickly overpower future adversaries. "Our forces in the next century must be agile, lethal, readily deployable, and require a minimum of logistical support," he declared. "On land, our heavy forces must be lighter [and] easier to deploy.... In the air, we must be able to strike from across the world with pinpoint accuracy.[68]

Once inaugurated as president, Bush ordered the Department of Defense to begin implementing the proposals originally articulated in the Citadel speech. "I have given [Defense Secretary Donald Rumsfeld] a broad mandate to challenge the status quo as we design a new architecture for the defense of America and our allies," Bush announced in early 2001. This new architecture would rely to a great extent on innovative technologies, but the emphasis would remain on the pursuit of enhanced "power projection."

These objectives have now been embedded in the Pentagon's long-range budgetary assumptions. Thus, in introducing the administration's $379 billion defense budget for fiscal year 2003 (an increase of $45 billion over fiscal year 2002), Secretary of Defense Rumsfeld declared, "We need rapidly deployable, fully integrated joint forces, capable of reaching distant theaters quickly and working with our air and sea forces to strike adversaries swiftly, successfully, and with devastating effect."[69] And while additional resources will also be devoted to missile defense and antiterrorism, this "power projection" mission will dominate U.S. military procurement and force development in the years ahead.

THE WAR ON TERROR

President Bush spelled out the broad outlines of the administration's third major priority, success in the war against terrorism, in his address to a joint session of Congress on September 20, nine days after the terror bombings in New York and Washington. "Our war on terror begins with al-Qaeda," he declared, but "it will not end until every terrorist group of global reach has been found, stopped, and defeated." This campaign would not be limited to a series of punitive strikes or one great battle, but would entail a "lengthy campaign," extending to many theaters of operation. To eliminate the threat of terrorism, moreover, military force would be used not only against terrorist cells and organizations, but also against states that housed or otherwise aided such entities.

This strategy entails two sorts of endeavors: first, an intelligence and law enforcement effort aimed at locating and destroying hidden terrorist cells; and second, a military effort aimed at destroying terrorist sanctuaries and punishing those states that offer them protection or assistance. While both endeavors are said to be crucial to the success of the war on terrorism, the military aspect of the campaign has attracted the greatest attention from senior administration officials and has been most closely associated with the two other key strands of American security policy.

Many aspects of the war in Afghanistan, for example, reflect the "power projection" model originally delineated by President Bush in his 1999 speech at the Citadel. In preparation for the Afghan campaign, the United States airlifted large amounts of weapons and equipment to friendly states in the area, and deployed a powerful naval fleet in the Arabian Sea. Light infantry forces carried out most of the fighting, supported by long-range bombers equipped with precision-guided weapons.

The Pentagon has applied this model to the invasion of Iraq. This operation has entailed the rapid insertion of tens of thousands of U.S. troops at strategic points around the country, along with relentless air and missile attacks.

The war on terrorism has also merged with the U.S. effort to safeguard access to key sources of petroleum, especially those in the Persian Gulf and the Caspian Sea basin. Indeed, the war in Afghanistan can be viewed as an extension of the shadow war in Saudi Arabia between radical opponents of the Saudi monarchy and the U.S.-backed royal family. Ever since King Fahd decided, in the wake of Iraq's August 1990 invasion of Kuwait, to allow U.S. troops to be deployed in his country and to use the kingdom as a base for attacks on Iraq, Saudi extremists led by Osama bin Laden have been fighting a subterranean war to topple the monarchy and drive the Americans out of the country. By the same token, American moves to destroy al-Qaeda and its support network in Afghanistan indirectly protect the Saudi royal family and thereby ensure access to Saudi oil supplies.[70]

As suggested earlier, the war on terrorism has also been merged with U.S. efforts to safeguard the flow of Caspian oil and natural gas to markets in the West. These efforts began on a modest scale during the Clinton administration, when the Department of Defense established links with the armed forces of Azerbaijan, Georgia, Kazakhstan, Kyrgyzstan, and Uzbekistan and began to provide them with military aid and training.[71] But now, in the wake of September 11, these efforts have been significantly expanded. Hence, the temporary U.S. bases in Uzbekistan and Kyrgyzstan are being transformed into semipermanent installations, while U.S. aid will be provided "for the refurbishment of a strategically located air base" in Kazakhstan. According to the State Department, this move is intended to "improve U.S.-Kazakh military cooperation while establishing a U.S.-interoperable base along the oil-rich Caspian."[72] Azerbaijan will use American aid to establish a maritime defense capability in the Caspian Sea—the site of several recent encounters between Azerbaijani oil-exploration vessels and Iranian gunboats. While facilitating these countries' participation in the war against terrorism, these initiatives are also linked to U.S. efforts to provide a safe environment for the production and transport of petroleum.[73]

THREE STRANDS, ONE ENTERPRISE

Whatever the original intent of American policy makers, the three key strands of the administration's foreign security policy—the pursuit of imported petroleum, the enhancement of U.S. "power projection" capabilities, and the war against terrorism—have now merged into a single strategic enterprise. Attempts to analyze these initiatives as separate phenomena will prove increasingly difficult as the three strands become more and more intertwined. The only way to accurately depict the overall thrust of U.S. security policy today is to speak of a unified campaign—"the war for American supremacy"—combining significant elements of all three strands.

It is probably much too early to gauge the long-term significance of this fusing of strategic priorities. But several preliminary observations can be offered. First, since it is very difficult to question a strategy that integrates so many key aspects of national security in a single unified campaign, the combined policy appears to possess more vigor and momentum than any of its constituent parts. It might be possible to impose limits on one aspect of the campaign, for example, reducing military procurement levels or U.S. troop deployments in certain oil regions. When these measures are combined with antiterrorism, however, it is almost impossible to advocate such limitations. It is highly likely, therefore, that the combined campaign will secure considerable support from Congress and the American people.

By the same token, however, this enterprise harbors a very significant risk of "mission creep" and "overstretch." That is, it could lead to a series of open-ended overseas military operations that become more complex and dangerous over time and require ever-growing commitments of American resources and personnel. George W. Bush warned against precisely this sort of behavior during the 2000 election campaign, but now seems to have embraced it fully. Certainly, this appears to be the case in the Persian Gulf, Central Asia, and Colombia, where the U.S. military presence is steadily being expanded. In each case, it is the *combined* impact of the three policy strands that makes it so difficult to establish prudent limits.

At this point, the greatest test of the Administration's overarching strategic design has come in Iraq. President Bush overthrew Saddam Hussein, after the Department of Defense spent months planning for the American invasion. Many Arab leaders warned the United States that such an invasion would trigger disorder and violence throughout the Middle East. Senior Pentagon officials also voiced concern over the costs and risks of maintaining a large American military presence in Iraq *after* Hussein has been ousted. But none of these warnings seem to have had any effect on the White House.

For those who worry about the long-term implications of the administration's strategic plan, the integration of these three strands of policy will pose a significant impediment to criticism. While it might be possible to convince some Americans and some members of Congress that U.S. military spending is too high or that energy consumption should be reduced, it will be very difficult to gain widespread support for this view while the war on terrorism is in full swing and the United States is becoming increasingly dependent on imported petroleum. Ultimately, it will be necessary to confront the "whole ball of wax"—that is, to question the desirability of the United States relying on military force to control the world's oil supply and to suppress all foreign challenges to American domination. The war for American supremacy will prove extremely costly in blood and treasure, and it will require ever more severe restrictions on civil liberties at home. In the final analysis, American democracy itself is put at the greatest risk by this strategy of perpetual intervention abroad.

MILITARY

by William D. Hartung

CONTRARY TO HIS campaign pledge to be more "humble" in pursuit of U.S. interests, George W. Bush has adopted an aggressive, unilateralist foreign policy that reflects unbridled imperial attitudes not seen since the peak period of direct U.S. interventionism in Latin America in the early decades of the twentieth century. But this time around, the overriding U.S. policy objective is to establish dominance on a global rather than a regional scale, and it is being pursued in a nuclear-armed world in which unchecked escalation or military miscalculation could lead to unprecedented destruction.

Under the guise of "modernizing" U.S. military forces and strategy, Bush policy makers have launched an undeclared war on international norms and the U.S. Constitution. From junking the Anti-Ballistic Missile Treaty to clear the way for missile defense and the militarization of space to declaring a doctrine of preemption to overthrow regimes the U.S. president deems threatening, the administration has moved relentlessly to destroy any and all obstacles to U.S. military intervention.[74]

In line with its desire for maximum freedom of action, the Bush administration has de-emphasized formal alliances and bilateral agreements in favor of what Secretary of Defense Donald Rumsfeld has described as "rotating coalitions" composed of nations that receive U.S. aid and arms in exchange for supporting short-term U.S. military objectives. In keeping with its focus on military force as the preeminent foreign policy tool, the Bush administration has launched the largest military buildup since the Reagan era, purchasing everything from Cold War–era combat ships and fighter planes to so-called transformational systems such as unmanned aerial vehicles and low-yield nuclear weapons. This strategy, largely in place before September 11, became a great deal easier to sell to Congress and the American public when the United States was on a war footing. The attacks on America and the subsequent inflation of external threats were a windfall for militarists, the Pentagon, and defense contractors.

RHETORIC AND REALITY

As a candidate for president, Bush promised to transform the U.S. military from a lumbering behemoth designed to fight a rival superpower that no longer exists into a more flexible, mobile force that could handle the multiple challenges of an unpredictable post–Cold War world.[75] To accomplish this goal, Bush pledged to scale back Cold War–era weapons to make way for a new generation of systems capable of striking accurately from long range without relying on large, vulnerable "platforms" like combat ships and heavy tanks.[76] Candidate Bush promised to accomplish this transition while increasing the Pentagon budget by as little as $45 billion over a ten-year period, less than half of the $100 billion, ten-year increase proposed by his Democratic rival, Al Gore. Bush's rhetoric of affordable transformation has not been borne out in reality. In the first nineteen months of his administration, Congress authorized over $150 billion in additional military spending. The military budget is approaching $400 billion per year, nearly one-third higher than it was when Bush took office.[77]

A casual observer might assume that this rapid acceleration in military spending was necessitated by the unexpected burdens of the "war on terrorism." But an analysis of the increased spending indicates that only about 25 percent of the $150 billion in new funding is directly related to fighting terrorism—either to pay the day-to-day costs of the war in Afghanistan or to stock up on heavily utilized items such as unmanned aerial vehicles (UAVs) and precision-guided bombs. The other 75 percent of the new funding is paying for Cold War–era weapons platforms that candidate Bush claimed would be cut back, or for new schemes like the president's ambitious missile defense program, which, despite the assertions of Star Wars boosters, bears no logical relationship to the task of fending off terrorist attacks.[78]

In short, Pentagon costs have not skyrocketed because of the war on terrorism, but because Secretary of Defense Donald Rumsfeld and his coterie have been unwilling to make hard choices that would upset powerful interests in the military-industrial-congressional complex. Rumsfeld's decision to cancel the Crusader artillery system is the exception that proves the rule: stopping the system frees up $9 billion, but that's only about 1 percent of the $850 billion the Pentagon has committed to major weapons systems already in the pipeline.[79]

The Bush administration's military buildup has been a bonanza for major defense contractors such as Lockheed Martin, Boeing, and Northrop Grumman, which were already receiving a total of $30 to $35 billion per year in Pentagon contracts. Not only will these major arms manufacturers be able to build lucrative Cold War–era systems, but they will benefit from new Pentagon investments in UAVs, long-range strike systems, and ballistic missile defense. And these same companies have received multibillion contracts for security work funded by other U.S. government agencies, such as the $11 billion Lockheed Martin-Northrop Grumman contract to re-arm and revitalize the U.S. Coast Guard and the major contracts that Boeing and Lockheed Martin have received for airport security systems.[80]

In addition to major spending increases, the biggest change in the Bush strategy is its ambitious pursuit of overwhelming military superiority. If this strategy is fully implemented, the major military spending increases of Bush's first two years in office will only be the down payment on a major buildup that could end up costing more than the Reagan administration's military spending binge of the 1980s.

PURSUING UNILATERAL SUPERIORITY

The first formal elaboration of the Bush administration's military strategy came with the QDR, which was released less than three weeks after the attacks on the Pentagon and the World Trade Center. The QDR, most of which was developed prior to the September 11 attacks, makes it clear that the Bush administration's aggressively interventionist strategy was already being developed before the advent of the war on terrorism.

The common thread that runs throughout the Defense Review is a fierce determination to maintain and expand global dominance. While defense debates during the 1990s frequently revolved around the question of whether the United States should downsize its global military commitments, the Bush-Rumsfeld strategy is clearly aimed at expanding U.S. global reach. In its summary of "enduring national interests," for example, the Defense Review speaks of the need to "preclude hostile domination of critical areas, particularly Europe, Northeast Asia, the East Asian littoral, and the Middle East and Southwest Asia." Add to that the declared interest in fostering "peace and stability in the Western Hemisphere" and the QDR's pledge to maintain "access to key markets and strategic resources" in Africa, and there is no major region that is *not* targeted by the new strategy.[81]

This "cover-the-globe" military strategy creates a requirement for access to additional bases and support facilities in key regions such as East Asia, supplemented by an effort to develop "systems capable of sustained operations at great distances with minimal theater-based support."[82] In search of a more flexible interventionary force, the new strategy shifts from the 1990s paradigm of preparing to fight and win major conflicts in Northeast and Southwest Asia simultaneously to a model based on a capability to "swiftly defeat aggression in overlapping major conflicts while preserving for the President the option to call for a decisive victory in one of these conflicts—*including the possibility of regime change or occupation* [emphasis added]."[83]

While the reference to "regime change or occupation" foreshadowed the Bush administration's overthrow of Saddam Hussein's regime in Iraq, another section of the Defense Review dealing with the dangers posed by "weak and failing states" suggests a rationale for ongoing U.S. intervention in Afghanistan or a future U.S. military engagement in a state like Somalia. The reference to fighting two "overlapping" conflicts, meanwhile, led some analysts to suggest that the Bush administration was reducing U.S. commitments relative to the previous objective of winning two major wars simultaneously. The Defense Review explicitly rejects this interpretation: "The United States is not abandoning planning for two conflicts to plan for fewer than two. On the contrary, DoD is changing the concept altogether by planning for victory across the spectrum of possible conflict."[85]

In September 2002, the aggressive strategy set out in the QDR was reinforced by the release of "The National Security Strategy of the United States," a popularized, thirty-one-page statement of the Bush administration's foreign policy priorities. Although the strategy document is filled with user-friendly rhetoric about the need to take "cooperative action" with other nations, the core message is even more ruthlessly unilateral than that of the QDR. The main thrust of the strategy document is that the Bush administration intends to exploit the "unprecedented—and unequaled—strength and influence of the United States" to implement a first strike military strategy.[86]

In a frequently quoted passage, the strategy statement asserts that "we will not hesitate to act alone, if necessary, to exercise our right of self-defense by acting preemptively… against terrorists." Similarly, the administration's primary response to the threat of nuclear weapons will not be non-proliferation or disarmament efforts but "counterproliferation"—the use of military force to "defend against the threat before it is unleashed." The spirit of the Bush strategy—which has the potential to unleash massive destruction in the name of defense—is summed up in a phrase that could just as easily be found on a Sunday afternoon football broadcast: "We recognize that our best defense is a good offense."[87]

SHOOT FIRST, ASK QUESTIONS LATER

In a June 2002 speech at West Point, President Bush unveiled his administration's new "doctrine of preemption," which holds that the United States reserves the right to attack any nation that may intend to harm the United States, whether or not an actual attack is imminent. It appeared that this new policy was designed to rationalize the administration's intended invasion of Iraq, once efforts to link Baghdad to the September 11 attacks or any other specific plan to attack the United States had proven unsuccessful.

As aggressive as it sounds in its own terms, the Bush doctrine actually goes well beyond preemption, which is generally understood to mean striking an adversary who is about to strike you. The Bush policy envisions taking military action against any regime that is deemed to be acting against U.S. interests, whether or not it is poised to attack the United States or its allies. The Bush policy could more accurately be called a first-strike policy or a "doctrine of unprovoked attack."

While the United States has engaged in military first strikes in the past, from the 1989 invasion of Panama to the invasion of Iraq, the Bush doctrine seeks to elevate this approach from an occasional tactic to a guiding principle of U.S. foreign policy. In addition, there are no stated limits to the new emphasis on these "preemptive" attacks, which could entail anything from "regime change" to a nuclear strike on suspected chemical or biological weapons facilities. The Pentagon is now calling for the rapid development of new systems such as a Mach-10 hypersonic missile that could be launched from space to hit targets anywhere on earth within minutes of the decision to attack.[88]

The likely side effect of this doctrine will be to legitimate the notion of striking first and to increase the possibility that a nation that fears an attack by the United States will seek to strike at U.S. forces or U.S. interests first, either openly or covertly. The notion of attacking another nation only in legitimate self-defense, a well-established principle of international law that has been violated far too often as it is, would be seriously undermined if the preemption doctrine were to become an enduring component of U.S. foreign policy.

NUCLEAR WEAPONS AND MISSILE DEFENSE

The Bush administration's nuclear doctrine, unveiled at the end of 2001 in the highly charged post–September 11 political climate, represents an abrupt departure from the policies of prior post–Cold War administrations, Republican and Democratic alike. These views are set out in the Nuclear Posture Review (NPR), which independent defense analyst William Arkin has described as "an integrated, significantly expanded planning doctrine for using nuclear weapons against a wide range of potential adversaries" that "reverses an almost two-decades-long trend of relegating nuclear weapons to the category of weapons of last resort."[89]

There are three particularly troubling aspects of the Bush nuclear doctrine. First, it expands the Pentagon's nuclear hit list by calling for detailed contingency plans for attacking a wide range of potential adversaries, whether or not those nations possess nuclear weapons. The Posture Review explicitly mentions China, Iran, Iraq, Libya, North Korea, Russia, and Syria, but they aren't necessarily the only targets. Second, the Bush approach expands the circumstances under which the use of nuclear weapons will be considered far beyond situations in which the national survival of the United States is at risk to include retaliation for a chemical or biological attack, an attack by Iraq on Israel or one of its neighbors, a North Korean attack on South Korea, a military conflict over the status of Taiwan, and even in response to "surprising military developments." Third, the administration is considering the creation of a new generation of more "usable" nuclear weapons, ranging from low-yield systems to use against hardened underground bunkers to nuclear warheads that can be fitted onto land-based missile interceptors as part of the administration's missile defense system.[90]

This latter approach, a multitiered missile defense system, would incorporate interceptors based on land, at sea, on aircraft, and eventually in outer space. While administration officials frequently give the impression that the system is meant to defend the United States from an unprovoked attack with a long-range ballistic missile, the system would most likely serve to back up a U.S. first strike against a state armed with ballistic missiles and some kind of weapon of mass destruction (nuclear, chemical, or biological). The missile defense system would be tasked to intercept any ballistic missiles that aren't destroyed in the initial U.S. attack, a potential sequence of events frequently referred to more euphemistically as a way to "preserve freedom of action" for the United States in a regional conflict involving North Korea or another potential nuclear-armed state.

Over the longer term, the missile defense program may be used as a stepping stone for the stationing of weapons in space, for purposes ranging from the protection of U.S. satellites to the targeting of adversaries on earth. The notion of space as the "new high frontier" that can assure U.S. military dominance for decades to come has been popular for some time in the U.S. Space Command and other outposts of the military bureaucracy.

As early as the mid-1990s, the U.S. Space Command's "Vision for 2020" spoke openly of "dominating the space dimension of military operations to protect U.S. interests and investments," with the ultimate goal of achieving "full spectrum dominance" on land, at sea, in the air, and in space.[91] The report suggests that the United States is "unlikely to be challenged by a global peer competitor," but that it should boost its military capabilities nonetheless, to deal with regional challenges spurred in part by "a widening between the 'haves' and 'have-nots'" driven by the "globalization of the world economy."[92] This bald-faced expression of celestial imperialism was questioned by many key leaders in the three traditional military services, who feared that it might undermine funding for more mundane forms of military power. But things are looking up for the advocates of space-based dominance. Donald Rumsfeld is the first secretary of defense to fully and enthusiastically embrace the notion that militarizing space is the key to maintaining unchallenged U.S. military superiority,[93] and he is not alone in his enthusiasms.[94]

To some degree, the dangers of the new nuclear doctrine have been obscured by the publicity accorded to the May 2002 Bush-Putin arms accord, under which Washington and Moscow have agreed to withdraw more than two-thirds of their strategic nuclear weapons from active deployment. Unfortunately, the agreement is so riddled with loopholes that it is more likely to stimulate rather than stifle nuclear weapons development. Neither side is required to destroy any of the nuclear weapons withdrawn from active service. The accord uses different counting rules than past arms accords, vastly overstating the levels of proposed cutbacks. Nothing in the agreement prevents either side from pursuing missile defenses or producing new nuclear weapons.

And either side can pull out of the treaty on just ninety days' notice.[95] From Washington's perspective, particularly after the U.S. withdrawal from the Anti-Ballistic Missile Treaty, the new agreement has more to do with buying off Russian President Vladimir Putin on the cheap and mollifying domestic public opinion than it does with pursuing enduring nuclear arms reductions.

BUYING ACCESS, BUYING ALLIES

The Bush administration's preference for unilateral solutions—or at best, ad hoc multilateral coalitions in which the United States makes all the key decisions—poses a serious challenge to its ambitious global strategy: How can the United States exert influence in every corner of the globe without resort to a massive increase in military personnel? So far, the solution has been to lavish arms, aid, and training on the allies of the moment in return for help in achieving U.S. objectives. Toward that end, in the early days of the war on terrorism, the administration floated a proposal that would have allowed the president to suspend for up to five years legislative restrictions on the provision of arms, aid, or training to any nation deemed an important partner in the war on terrorism. Congress quickly rebuffed this across-the-board approach, which would have bypassed restrictions based on human rights abuses, subversion of democracy, sponsorship of terrorism, proliferation of nuclear weapons, or any other reason. But the administration was able to win support for a bill lifting most of the sanctions against India and Pakistan based on their potential roles as key players in the U.S.-led war in Afghanistan.

In the first year after September 11, the United States offered arms and training to India, Pakistan, Yemen, Qatar, the former Soviet Republic of Georgia, Uzbekistan,

Tajikistan, the Philippines, and Indonesia based on their potential roles in fighting terrorism in their own nations or in neighboring countries. As a result, U.S. military aid spending increased by 28 percent from FY 2001 to FY 2002, while funds for training of foreign military forces have increased by more than one-third.[96] In the majority of cases, this U.S. aid has more than one purpose. In addition to whatever value a particular arms deal or training mission may have in combating al-Qaeda or other "terror networks of global reach" as President Bush has described them, it may also serve as a way to secure access to military facilities (the Philippines, Uzbekistan, Tajikistan, Qatar) or to develop relationships with military forces in regions of interest (Yemen, Georgia) as a way to facilitate U.S. intervention.

The Clinton and Bush Sr. administrations pursued this policy of swapping aid, arms, and training for access and influence, but the current administration has been more aggressive in reopening or expanding supply relationships with nations that have questionable human rights records, such as Uzbekistan and Indonesia.[97] The Bush administration has also engaged in extensive covert arms shipments to warlords in Afghanistan, first as a way of putting pressure on the Taliban, and then in exchange for assistance in tracking down Taliban and al-Qaeda operatives. U.S. allies and aid officials in Afghanistan have suggested that this continuing arms supply relationship is bolstering the power of unaccountable warlords at the expense of Afghanistan's fledgling coalition government, but so far these concerns have fallen on deaf ears in the Bush administration.[98]

PREVENTION, NOT INTERVENTION

Rather than promoting a first-strike doctrine that will escalate global tensions and increase the likelihood of conflict,

Military Aid to the New Allies in the War on Terrorism

Country	2001	2003
Armenia	0	3,750
Azerbijan	0	3,750
Ethiopia	0	1,000
Georgia	4,971	8,200
India	498	51,000
Indonesia	0	400
Jordan	76,535	200,400
Kazakhstan	2,479	4,000
Krygyzstan	2,226	5,100
Kenya	1,443	2,100
Nepal	237	3,500
Oman	250	20,750
Pakistan	0	51,000
Philippines	3,431	22,400
Tajikistan	0	350
Turkey	1,689	20,300
Uzbekistan	2,939	9,950
Yemen	198	2,650
Total	96,698	410,600

Note: Military aid includes Foreign Military Financing and International Military Education and Training.

Source: Department of State, FY 2003 *Congressional Budget Justification for Foreign Operations* (Washington, DC: Department of State, April 15,2002), pp. 505-524.

U.S. policy should be based on preventing the spread of weapons of mass destruction and reducing the likelihood of conflict. This will require the use of many of the diplomatic, economic, and political tools that the Bush administration has cast aside in its ill-considered drive for permanent military superiority. The Bush administration's disastrous mishandling of nuclear arms diplomacy with North Korea is an object lesson in the limits of its first-strike doctrine for dealing with real-world threats of nuclear proliferation. Pyongyang's threats to restart its nuclear weapons program and abandon the Nuclear Non-Proliferation Treaty came after almost two years of provocation from the Bush administration, which denounced Pyongyang as part of the "axis of evil" and refused to follow through on commitments made by the Clinton administration under the 1994 U.S.–North Korea nuclear framework agreement.[99]

As a first step toward demilitarizing U.S. foreign policy, a preventive strategy would restructure the U.S. military as a defensive force capable of fighting one major conflict plus engaging in peacekeeping operations. As Admiral William Owens (USN, Ret.) noted in an interview just after the September 11 attacks, given the proper strategy and priorities, the United States could be better defended with a $200 billion Pentagon budget than a budget of $300 billion and beyond.[100] With military spending now consuming more than half of federal discretionary outlays, this strategy shift would also free up funds for education, environmental protection, housing, transportation, and other necessary components of a strong and resilient society. Finally, as an investment in global stability, the United States should cut back the $7 to $8 billion per year it spends subsidizing weapons exports while increasing nonmilitary foreign aid from 0.1 to 0.7 percent of gross domestic product.

A preventive strategy should also include a pledge to abide by existing multilateral treaties designed to stop the spread of nuclear, biological, and chemical weapons. The United States should also use its considerable political and financial resources to help strengthen the monitoring, verification, and enforcement of these agreements. In keeping with the U.S. obligation to take urgent steps to eliminate its

Bush administration has rejected that vision, resulting in the unparalleled U.S. renunciation of international law and international treaties.

SHREDDING THE UN CHARTER'S PROHIBITION ON THE USE OF FORCE

The Bush administration has decided to openly challenge the UN Charter. The Charter's core principle, contained in Article 2(4) and Article 51, proscribes one nation from attacking another except in self-defense. In a speech to the graduating class at West Point in June 2002, Bush set forth a doctrine that repudiated this critical legal principle. Building on his State of the Union address, in which he warned the "axis of evil" nations that the United States would not wait "while dangers gather," he articulated a doctrine of preemptive strikes. This radically new approach proclaims that the United States can use military force against any state it perceives to be hostile, or that seeks to acquire biological, chemical or nuclear weapons, or is viewed as aiding terrorism.[103]

This new U.S. position, obviously aimed at justifying an attack on Iraq, is a public renunciation of the UN Charter's norm that force not be used except in response to an attack by another nation. Although both the Soviet Union and the United States invaded countries during the forty-year Cold War to further perceived national interest—the Soviet interventions in Hungary, Czechoslovakia, and Afghanistan; and the U.S. military incursions into Cuba, the Dominican Republic, Nicaragua, Grenada, Libya, and Panama—both superpowers maintained a formal fealty to the Charter's proscription on the use of force except in self-defense. The United States traditionally sought to avoid sweeping justifications for its attacks on other countries that would have essentially eviscerated the Charter's norm. Instead, past administrations sought to expand the self-defense exception, stretching its parameters to the breaking point to justify what seemed clearly illegal, but not obliterating its core.

Preemptive strikes should be distinguished from an earlier doctrine that was labeled "anticipatory self-defense" under which the United States and some other countries argued that they had the right under the UN Charter to attack a country that was planning an attack. This latter doctrine at least gave lip service to the restrictions on the use of force embodied in the Charter—that force could only be used in self-defense or as authorized by the Security Council under Article 51. The new doctrine of preemptive strikes moves beyond the restrictions of the Charter by stating that force will be used even if there is no immediate threat. Past administrations publicly viewed preemptive strikes on other nations as illegal. Even the Reagan administration joined the Security Council in unanimously condemning Israel's attack on Iraq's nuclear facility in 1981. Only after the Cold War's demise did the Clinton administration come close to breaking with the Charter's norms when NATO attacked Yugoslavia in response to the Kosovo crisis. In this case, however, the United States declined to put forth a new doctrine of humanitarian military interventions, choosing to characterize Kosovo as an exceptional emergency. The new Bush doctrine may well take the world back to a period prior to World War I when the employment of force had no legal restraints; countries could use force when and where they wanted.

As a candidate, Bush spoke of "humility" in defining America's role in the world. Now, articulating a more imperial vision than any prior president dared publicly articulate, the administration proposes abandoning the UN Charter's core legal restraint in favor of a system in which the United States unilaterally decides which regimes warrant replacement by force. The consequences of this new doctrine are frightening. Once the United States so publicly undermines the Charter, what will prevent other nations from preemptively striking their enemies when they perceive such an attack to be in their national interest? This new assertion of the right to use force, contrary to the UN Charter, is the most dangerous and serious of the Bush administration's dismissal of the international legal framework.

SCUTTLING THE INTERNATIONAL CRIMINAL COURT

Another area that illustrates the Bush administration's disrespect for international agreements and its unilateral approach to foreign policy is the decision to renounce the Rome Treaty establishing the ICC. The Nuremberg trials after World War II set in motion efforts by progressive nations and nongovernmental organizations to establish an international criminal court to hold accountable individuals who commit genocide, war crimes, or crimes against humanity. These efforts finally succeeded in the Rome Conference in 1998, which, according to Article 5 of the ICC Statute, established a court to try "the most serious crimes of concern to the international community as a whole."

The Clinton administration's attitude to the establishment of the Court was mixed. The United States had backed ad-hoc international tribunals to try war crimes committed in the former Yugoslavia and Rwanda. In 1995 it generally supported the idea of a permanent court. However, the Clinton administration sought to ensure that no American would ever be tried by such a court without the consent of the U.S. government. The United States argued that its unique role in the world required that protections be accorded to American soldiers. It proposed that only the Security Council refer cases to the Court, a proposal ensuring that the U.S. veto on the Security Council could block any prosecution of

American soldiers or civilians. The overwhelming majority of states at the Rome Conference rejected this proposal.

The Clinton administration was dissatisfied with the compromises that eventually were adopted at the Rome Conference.[104] For example, the final treaty allows the Security Council to delay a prosecution by a vote of nine of its fifteen members, but did not give the United States a veto over such prosecutions. Nonetheless, Clinton signed the treaty on December 31, 2000 with the expectation that modifications would be negotiated before submission of the treaty to the Senate for ratification.

The Bush administration backed away from the Clinton policy of continuing to negotiate within the treaty's framework. Instead, on May 6, 2002, the administration took the more radical step of announcing that it would unsign the Rome Treaty. Using the antiterrorism specter to justify this radical step, Secretary of Defense Donald Rumsfeld stated that "there is a risk that the ICC could attempt to assert jurisdiction over U.S. service members, as well as civilians, involved in counterterrorist and other military operations— something we cannot allow."[105] Despite U.S. objections, eighty-seven countries, including most of our European allies, had by January 2003 ratified the treaty, and the Court is in the process of being established.

Of course, the ICC would be a good way to bring terrorists to justice. Had it been in existence at the time, the Court could have handled the alleged perpetrators of the September 11 attacks, including Osama bin Laden. Perhaps the war with Afghanistan would have been avoided. The international community would have considered trials before the ICC as fairer than trials in U.S. courts, particularly trials before military commissions. By attempting to scuttle the Court, the United States is removing an important deterrent to terrorism.

In spring 2002, the United States threatened to veto UN peacekeeping missions unless U.S. troops in those missions were accorded absolute immunity from prosecution by the ICC. The fifteen members of the European Union and most other countries of the world opposed U.S. efforts to undermine the basic principles of the ICC. As the Canadian ambassador to the UN Paul Heinbecker stated, "Fundamental principles of international law and the place of those principles in the conduct of global affairs are in question."[106] Eventually, a temporary Security Council compromise providing American troops in those missions a one-year immunity was worked out, a vote that the Canadian ambassador called "a sad day for the UN."[107]

The United States is using an additional tactic: it is asking signatories to the treaty to sign separate agreements certifying that they will not extradite Americans for trial before the ICC. A commission of the European Union considers such bilateral agreements illegal and against the object and purpose of the ICC treaty. By January 2003, seventeen countries—including Romania, Israel, India, East Timor, and Tajikistan—had signed such special treaties to ensure an unrestricted flow of U.S. military assistance. In addition, the Bush administration has served notice that the U.S. role in NATO will change unless European countries agree not to extradite Americans.

DISREGARDING THE GENEVA CONVENTIONS

While the UN Charter sets forth a framework to preserve international peace, the Geneva Conventions provide protections to combatants, civilians, the wounded, and prisoners of war (POWs) once war breaks out. The U.S. treatment of prisoners captured during the war in Afghanistan openly violates the Geneva Conventions and is raising concerns throughout the world. The United States has refused to give any of those captured in Afghanistan the rights to which prisoners of war are entitled. Instead, it has imprisoned over five hundred people from some thirty-three countries in a prison at a U.S. military base in Guantanamo Bay, Cuba. It has charged none of these persons with a crime, claims the right to keep them imprisoned indefinitely, and is arguing, so far successfully, that no court can review the imprisonments. It is refusing to allow these prisoners access to their families or lawyers.

Under the Geneva Conventions, captured combatants are entitled to treatment as POWs; if there is any doubt with regard to that status, they are entitled to a hearing before a competent tribunal, as mandated by the Third Geneva Convention.[108] According to the International Committee of the Red Cross, which monitors the Geneva Conventions, such tribunals should have been held for all Guantanamo combatants not considered POWs.[109] The Inter-American Commission on Human Rights of the Organization of American States recently upheld the principle that a tribunal or court determines the status and rights of the Guantanamo detainees. On March 13, 2002, the Commission, concerned that petitioners were "entirely at the unfettered discretion of the United States government," asked the United States "to take the urgent measures necessary to have the legal status of the detainees at Guantanamo Bay determined by a competent tribunal."[110] The United States, in violation of international law, refused to take such measures.

But the question goes far beyond the treatment of individual detainees at Guantanamo. Rather, it sets the stage for how, in a violent world, the rules of war are established for everyone. The United States has always argued for a broad reading of the Geneva and Hague Conventions regarding POWs, both to set an example and to ensure fair treatment of its own soldiers when captured. The United States has an immediate and long-term interest in upholding international conventions that establish universal rules of war and regulate the treatment of POWs. Our own soldiers live under the threat of capture and deserve the protection of the Geneva Conventions. The United States also has an interest in not alienating its battlefield allies with high-handed, unilateral decision making and selective compliance with the law. If the rules of war can be abrogated at any moment on the whim of the secretary of defense, our ability to form solid and lasting alliances will be gravely undercut.

AN END TO MULTILATERAL TREATIES

The Clinton administration had a mixed record with regard to treaty signing and ratification. Clinton did sign the ICC treaty as well as the Comprehensive Test Ban Treaty (CTBT), but the Senate never voted on the former and rejected the latter. The administration refused to sign or take to the Senate for ratification the treaty banning the production and use of antipersonnel mines. However, it did plan to eliminate antipersonnel mines by 2003 except in Korea, and, if alternatives were found, it planned to eliminate all land mines by 2006 (by mid-2002, this commitment as well was in doubt as the Bush administration reviewed its landmine policy). In 1998, the Clinton administration signed the Kyoto agreement that would have mandated reductions in "greenhouse gases" that contribute to global warming, but the Senate never ratified the treaty. Thus, while the Clinton administration was not exactly receptive to a number of treaties and showed signs of unilateral superpowerism, it signed a number of them, indicating it would not take actions hostile to the goals and aims of the treaties and in the hope of continuing to negotiate for better terms. By signing, it was at least giving a nod to multilateral solutions to international problems.

The Bush administration has taken a far more unilateral and hostile attitude to multilateral treaties, international institutions, and even global meetings such as the World Conference Against Racism and the World Food Summit. It has taken off its gloves and does not even pretend to engage in multilateralism; it is engaging in a naked exercise of power. The administration rejected the 1997 Kyoto Protocol, calling it "fatally flawed" and not in the "economic interest" of the United States. While the European Union has recently completed ratification of the treaty, the United States has announced that it will not even consider the multilateral climate treaty for at least ten years and will not participate in treaty talks scheduled for 2005 to reduce those gases. The United States, the greatest producer of greenhouse gases, will not reduce its levels under Bush's unilateral plan. In addition, the U.S. refusal will encourage other countries to do likewise in order to compete with the United States without restrictions on their own emissions.

The Bush administration has announced its opposition to the CTBT, which was ratified by all of our NATO allies and by Russia, but rejected by the Senate in 1999. This treaty mandates negotiations that would ultimately lead to nuclear disarmament. The administration will not resubmit the treaty to the Senate, thus seriously jeopardizing nuclear disarmament not only by the United States, but by other states as well. In December 2001 the Bush administration gave Russia the required six-month notice that it was abrogating the Anti-Ballistic Missile Treaty in order to develop its "Star Wars" missile defense system. The abrogation of the treaty was not authorized under its terms—there were no extraordinary events that jeopardized U.S. interests. In addition, there is a serious question whether Bush could abrogate the treaty without the consent of Congress. This is the first time a major power has withdrawn from a nuclear arms control treaty. When coupled with the Bush position on the CTBT it is indeed ominous—we may well be entering a period of escalation in the nuclear arms race with all of the danger that entails.

In November 2001 the administration abruptly killed a many-year effort to negotiate a verification protocol that would have given teeth to the Biological Weapons Convention. The move reflected the Bush administration's deep suspicion of multilateral arms agreements, and the administration argued that it was pointless to negotiate with governments aggressively seeking biological weapons. Defense officials and the U.S. biotech industry had long opposed opening their own labs to international inspection. As one UK official said, "[T]he failure of the international community to agree to a protocol on biological weapons is a disaster."[111]

We are indeed in a time of great jeopardy. Yes, the world is a dangerous place, but it is also increasingly interconnected and plagued by transnational crises that require cooperative solutions. Without effective international institutions, adherence to existing treaties, and bold new treaties, our safety and climate are facing threats that are even more serious. Problems such as global warming, the use of force, the mistreatment of prisoners of war, and the proliferation of nuclear weapons affect all of us; even a superpower is not exempt, for global problems cannot be solved unilaterally. Unfortunately, the United States has not followed the path of greater cooperation, whether under Clinton or Bush. Recent actions by the Bush administration are diametrically opposed to a world based upon law, not power. The administration has placed the United States literally above the law and in so doing has endangered us all.

FOREIGN ECONOMIC POLICY
by Mark Weisbrot

"WE FIGHT AGAINST POVERTY because hope is an answer to terror," President Bush said in March 2002 when announcing an increase in foreign aid.[112] Two months later, the rock band U2's lead singer, Bono, and Treasury Secretary Paul O'Neill took a ten-day tour of Africa to witness the ravages of poverty and disease.

Despite the public relations fluff of the Africa tour and a proposed 38 percent increase in foreign economic aid by 2006, the Bush administration did not opt for a less destructive foreign economic policy in order to win allies in its "war on terrorism." The increase in aid, for instance, won't kick in until 2004 and still leaves the United States dead last among industrialized countries in terms of international giving as a percentage of GNP. The Africa tour resulted in no new initiatives. Contributions to strategic allies linked to the "war on terrorism" have been heavily focused on military assistance, for instance nearly $400 million in additional foreign military financing for such countries as Pakistan, Yemen, and Turkey.

The administration also took advantage of September 11 to squeeze fast-track authority—negotiating new commercial trade agreements with only an up-or-down vote—through the House of Representatives by only one vote. Speaker Dennis Hastert (R-IL) warned the House just before the vote that "[t]his Congress will either support our president who is fighting a courageous war on terrorism and redefining American world leadership or we will undercut this president at the worst possible time."[113]

As noted throughout this book, the Bush administration is widely seen as having a less civilized, more unilateral approach to foreign policy, representing a significant step backward from the previous administration. Whatever the merits of this argument in the overall realm of foreign policy, it certainly does not apply to foreign economic policy. In this area, continuity with the previous administration's policies around lending, trade, and aid is very strong—in spite of September 11.

CREDITORS' CARTEL

To understand both the continuity and the minor change requires an examination in detail of the institutions through which the United States exercises control over developing countries and shapes the framework in which international commerce takes place. These institutions are, in order of power and importance, the International Monetary Fund (IMF), the World Bank, and the World Trade Organization (WTO). These are ostensibly multilateral institutions, but it is well known that the IMF is primarily controlled by the U.S. Treasury Department.[114] The World Bank is subordinate to the IMF, and most other lenders—including the governments of the major industrialized powers and even much of the private sector—defer to the IMF's judgment.

This creditors' cartel, in conjunction with what Columbia economist Jagdish Bhagwati has called the "Wall Street–Treasury complex," confronts most low- and middle-income countries with enormous power. It is analogous to the power that the Oil Producing and Exporting Countries (OPEC) have over oil. OPEC uses its cartel to control, as much as possible, the price of oil; the IMF/Treasury uses the creditors' cartel not to control the price of credit, but to decide the economic (and sometimes political) policies of borrowing countries.

In other words, the IMF is able to tell most governments that if they do not adopt its policies, then they will not get credit from most other sources. This is the most concentrated power in the world, greater in its efficacy than the might of the U.S. military. Very few governments of low- and middle-income countries are strong enough (politically or economically) to stand up to this kind of power. As a result, the United States only rarely needs to use force or the threat of force, because it is able to impose its agenda by means of this cartel.[115]

This agenda has been enormously destructive in terms of its economic and social cost. There has been a sharp slowdown in economic growth over the last twenty years in the vast majority of low- and middle-income countries. For example, income per person grew by 75 percent in Latin America from 1960 to1980; from 1980 to 2000 it grew by only 7 percent.[116] As would be expected during a time of severely reduced economic growth, progress on the major social indicators such as life expectancy, infant and child mortality, literacy, and education has also slowed considerably. The major exceptions to these trends are those countries that were able to pursue economic policies independent of, and distinct from, those recommended by the IMF/Treasury cartel, such as China and India.

In some cases the cartel acts as a debt collector for the major banks and financial institutions. During the Asian financial crisis, for instance, the IMF persuaded the government of South Korea to guarantee billions of dollars of bad loans made by foreign banks. More destructive, the cartel pursues policies that even the multinational banks and corporations could not by themselves enforce or be interested in enforcing, including high interest rates that strangle economic growth, inappropriate exchange rate regimes (as in Russia and Brazil in 1998–99, and Argentina until 2001), and fiscal austerity even in the face of recession or depression. Over the last twenty years, the replacement of country-specific industrial or agricultural policies with a simple formula of opening up the domestic economy to international trade and capital flows has precluded most of the developing world from catching up, as South Korea and Taiwan have done, with the living standards of more developed countries. And in those cases where the Fund and allied economists have been given even more of a free hand, such as the "transition" economies, the results have been even more catastrophic. Russia lost about half its national income in the early to mid-1990s, the worst economic failure on record outside of wars and natural disasters.[117]

Even among progressive thinkers critical of U.S. foreign economic policies and the IMF/World Bank, the damage caused by these institutions and their policies is underestimated, because many people do not understand the importance of economic growth. For example, in countries in which poverty has increased or where progress in reducing poverty has slowed, the major cause has been the slowdown in economic growth, rather than changes in distribution of income or wealth. In the last twenty years, growth in all the low- and middle-income countries combined has been about half of its rate during the previous two decades (1960–1980).

LENDING

During the 1990s, Treasury Secretaries Robert Rubin and (especially) Larry Summers of the Clinton administration were aggressive advocates for the IMF and for using its power to break open foreign markets for both capital and goods. In so doing they caused enormous economic destruction. For example, the Asian financial crisis was mainly brought on by the removal of restrictions on portfolio investment, at Treasury's urging, which led in 1996 to a reversal of capital flows of $105 billion (11 percent of the GDP of South Korea,

Thailand, Indonesia, Malaysia, and the Philippines). In the wake of the crisis, the IMF conditioned their loans on the removal of restrictions on foreign direct investment into what had been protected national markets.[118]

The current administration has a more mixed attitude toward this kind of IMF and World Bank lending. Undersecretary of the Treasury for International Affairs John Taylor and White House Chief Economic Adviser Lawrence Lindsey hail from a more libertarian tradition than their predecessors. During Taylor's time at Stanford University, he advocated the abolition of the IMF.[119] Together with Treasury Secretary O'Neill, this group opposes "bailouts," even if it means that U.S. banks and other creditors suffer greater losses in a crisis situation. These "bailouts" generally do more harm than good, as in the case of the Asian bailout (the biggest ever at $120 billion), from which the largest economy, Indonesia, has still not recovered. Thus this faction within the administration is potentially a positive influence, at least with regard to this issue.

In practice, however, more traditional voices seem to prevail. Consider the most recent $30 billion loan to Brazil. This will help major U.S. banks such as Citigroup, FleetBoston, and J. P. Morgan Chase, who have $25.6 billion in loans to Brazil, get their money out under more favorable conditions. It was also designed to postpone the inevitable default until after the October 2002 election, to use the threat of default against the new president and lock him into current policies with future disbursements.[120] The winner of this election, Luiz Inacio (Lula) da Silva of the Workers Party, represents a clear break with the "Washington consensus." Nonetheless the Bush administration took a less interventionist stance toward the election than the Clinton administration did in the previous race in 1998, in which the United States made a $40 billion loan agreement contingent on President Fernando Henrique Cardoso's reelection.[121]

In Argentina, the creditors' cartel has been quite brutal, dragging out negotiations for a loan agreement for more than eight months since the default in December 2001, moving the goalposts as the government has caved in to one politically unpopular (and often economically harmful) demand after another.[122] It is not clear whether, as George Soros has suggested, the Fund is seeking to punish Argentina for the largest default on public debt ($141 billion) in history, so as to discourage other defaults,[123] or whether the failure to reach an agreement is a result of conflicts among IMF, U.S. Treasury, and White House decision makers. Nevertheless the prolonged negotiations, during which the government has been unable to adopt any economic stimulus program, have inflicted considerable damage on Argentina, whose economic collapse is very clearly a result of failed policies that received tens of billions of dollars worth of support from Washington.[124] Any new loans would go to pay existing official creditors, and the conditions attached to them (e.g., fiscal and monetary austerity) would prolong and/or worsen the country's severe economic depression.[125]

Aside from the bailouts, IMF and World Bank lending has followed a familiar pattern in the Bush era, with conditions supporting privatization, trade liberalization, and unnecessary fiscal and monetary austerity.

TRADE

Although there were some very minor concessions in the latest round of WTO negotiations regarding the issue of patents on essential medicines, the Bush administration has maintained the same positions on trade—and trade-related institutions such as the WTO—as its predecessor. These policies—on trade liberalization, international investment, and intellectual property rights—have contributed over the last two decades to the sharp slowdown in growth experienced by most developing countries, and to the large upward redistribution of income in the United States.

The administration continues to pursue the extension of U.S. patent and copyright law to the rest of the world as perhaps its most important foreign commercial policy objective. This policy has resulted in the denial of access to essential medicines to those who will die as a result, including many of the 40 million people in developing countries who have AIDS or are HIV positive. The enforcement and extension of intellectual property protection—including patents, copyrights, and royalties—also causes an enormous drain of resources from poor to rich countries, perhaps matching the total development assistance from North to South.[126] Although political contributions from pharmaceutical companies are now heavily skewed toward Republicans,[127] it is worth noting that the administration has made no attempt to roll back concessions—such as grudging acceptance of Brazilian and South African laws on generic AIDS drugs—that were won from the Clinton administration through organized protest and international opposition.[128]

On regional trade pacts, Bush has simply continued Clinton's policies, even winning the fast-track authority unsuccessfully sought by his predecessor. These policies, even according to the research of economists that support them, have contributed significantly to one of the most massive upward redistributions of income in American history in which the majority of the labor force has failed to share in the gains from economic growth over more than a quarter century.[129] The real median wage in the United States in 2000 was less than 4 percent over its 1973 level, despite a 72 percent increase in income per person during this period. It will be difficult to reverse this trend so long as new commercial agreements—such as the proposed Free Trade of the Americas Agreement, which would extend NAFTA to thirty-one countries—continue to throw U.S. workers into increasing competition with their counterparts earning as little as one dollar a day, and increase the power of multinational corporations over their employees.

The creditors' cartel consistently pressures low- and middle-income countries to open their markets to goods, services, and capital from the rich countries, while the latter maintain trade barriers of their own in agriculture and for certain manufactured goods. This double standard has recently become a sore spot among leaders of some developing countries, and a significant issue in the press. However, even according to the World Bank's own models, the impact on developing countries of access to rich countries' markets is quite small. According to the Bank, if the developed countries removed all of their barriers to merchandise trade, including steel, agricultural goods, and textiles—phased in by 2015—the net gain to the low- and middle-income countries would be about 0.6 percent of gross domestic product. In other words, the average person in sub-Saharan Africa making five hundred dollars a year would, as a result of this trade liberalization, make an additional three dollars annually.[130] The whole debate about market access is therefore mostly a distraction from the real issues of poverty, growth, and development.

DEBT AND THE DOLLAR

Most of the countries that have gotten debt relief through the Heavily Indebted Poor Countries (HIPC) Initiative launched in 1996 are still paying more for debt service than for health care and education and are plagued by harmful conditions attached to the debt relief. The Bush administration has continued this initiative, and the process of approving countries for debt relief has accelerated. But six years after the launching of HIPC, only four of forty-one countries have reached the "completion point" at which the full amount of pledged debt relief is granted.

One positive change proposed by the current administration was to convert up to 50 percent of the World Bank's lending to poor countries from loans to grants. This would have lowered the long-term debt burden of poor countries and reduced the Bank's leverage over them. The Bank strenuously resisted this change, correctly seeing it as something that would reduce its power, and—together with some liberal NGOs—persuaded some European governments to oppose Washington on this issue. Over the last fifty-seven years, Europe has almost never publicly opposed the United States on World Bank or IMF policy. The result was a compromise.[131]

The Clinton administration supported a "strong dollar" policy that favored the financial sector over the rest of the economy, led to record trade and current account deficits in recent years, contributed to the loss of manufacturing jobs and to wage inequality in the United States, and caused the foreign debt burden to grow at an unsustainable rate. Treasury Secretary O'Neill, who comes from a manufacturing background, has mostly gone along with this but appears less enthusiastic. The dollar's inevitable decline began in 2002. The Bush administration may be somewhat less likely to cause further harm by trying to prevent this; although it might also defer to Wall Street and the Federal Reserve (which favors a higher dollar because it helps to keep inflation lower).

CONCLUSION

It would be extremely difficult for the Bush administration to match the economic harm caused by the Clinton administration's foreign commercial policy, but that is largely because of greater public awareness. When NAFTA passed Congress in 1994, hardly anyone noticed its Chapter 11 clause, which gave corporations the right for the first time to sue governments directly over environmental and other regulations that infringed on their profits. Similarly, Congress approved the WTO agreement the next year with little public debate, and even the demonstrators at Seattle in 1999 did not fully realize the awful significance of the agreement's provisions on intellectual property rights.

To the extent that the Bush administration differs from its predecessors on foreign economic policy, it is mainly because of officials such as Lindsey, Taylor, and O'Neill, who represent a minority faction (in terms of influence) in the Republican Party.[132] This faction is less interested in protecting the power of such institutions as the IMF and World Bank and using them to determine the economic policies of developing countries. So far, they have not changed much in this regard. But in any case, there is little basis for expecting the Bush administration to pursue foreign economic policies that are significantly worse—or better—than those of its predecessors.

Nonetheless, there has been continued progress in the public debate, with some prominent economists winning over a wider audience with critiques of neoliberalism and the Washington consensus, and making some headway in the press. Leading the charge has been 2001 Nobel Prize winner Joseph Stiglitz.[133] In August 2002, Paul Krugman, a distinguished economist with a regular column in the *New York Times*, noted for the first time in that paper that the average person in Latin America was probably worse off than in 1980, and he announced his second thoughts: "I, too, bought into much though not all of the Washington consensus...my confidence that we've been giving good advice is way down."[134]

Neoliberalism has been so thoroughly disgraced in Latin America that even those who have implemented these polices for years, such as ruling party candidate Jose Serra in Brazil who lost to Lula, had to campaign against their past policies. And the collapse of the stock market in the United States, followed by the wave of accounting and corporate governance scandals, has discredited the "American

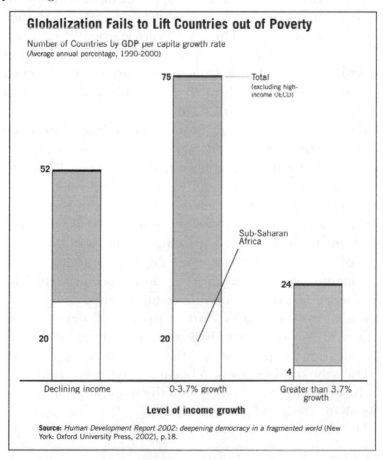

Globalization Fails to Lift Countries out of Poverty

Number of Countries by GDP per capita growth rate
(Average annual percentage, 1990-2000)

Source: *Human Development Report 2002: deepening democracy in a fragmented world* (New York: Oxford University Press, 2002), p.18.

model" in Europe, Asia, and other places where just two years ago it was being emulated to usher in a host of deregulatory and antilabor "reforms." All this has not yet translated into political progress, but it almost certainly will in the near future.

INTELLIGENCE
by Mel Goodman

ONE WEEK AFTER the attack on the Pentagon and the World Trade Center, National Security Adviser Condoleezza Rice told the press corps, "This isn't Pearl Harbor." No, it was worse. Sixty years ago, the United States did not have a director of central intelligence or thirteen intelligence agencies or a combined intelligence budget of more than $30 billion to provide early warning of enemy attack.

There is another significant and telling difference between Pearl Harbor and September 11. Less than two weeks after the surprise attack on Pearl Harbor, President Franklin D. Roosevelt appointed a high-level military and civilian commission to determine the causes of the intelligence failure. Following the September attacks, however, President Bush, CIA director George Tenet, and the chairmen of the Senate and House intelligence committees were adamantly opposed to any investigation or postmortem. The president's failure to appoint a statutory inspector general at the CIA from January 2001 to April 2002 deprived the agency of the one individual who could have started an investigation regardless of the director's opposition. Overall, the unwillingness to begin a congressional inquiry for nearly eight months increased the suspicion that indicators of an attack had gone unheeded.

The eventual Senate and House intelligence committee

investigation of the September 11 failure, which began in June 2002, was mishandled from the beginning. The original staff director for the investigation, former CIA inspector general Britt Snider, had the stature and experience for the job, but he was soon pushed out by former Senate intelligence committee chairman Richard Shelby (R-GA), a staunch critic of CIA Director Tenet but never an advocate for reform of the intelligence community. The staff itself is too small and inexperienced to do the job seriously. The August 2002 decision of the chairmen of the Senate and House intelligence committees to order an aggressive FBI investigation of the joint committee, ostensibly to uncover leaks of classified information, marked a blatant violation of the separation of powers between the executive and legislative branches.[135] The move was designed to placate the Bush administration, which has consistently established roadblocks to an independent investigation of the intelligence community.

Nevertheless, the preliminary report of the joint intelligence committee has done an excellent job of ferreting out evidence documenting the failures at the CIA and the FBI. The report describes a director of central intelligence who declared a war on terrorism in 1998 but allocated no additional funding or personnel to the task force on terrorism; an intelligence community that never catalogued information on the use of airplanes as weapons; and a CIA that refused to acknowledge the possibility of weaponizing commercial aircraft for terrorism until two months after the attacks on the World Trade Center and the Pentagon.[136] Two days after the report was published, the Bush administration reversed itself and endorsed the creation of a separate, independent investigation to study the intelligence failure.[137]

FAILURES OF INTELLIGENCE

The failure to anticipate the September 11 attack—and the reluctance to thoroughly investigate this failure—is merely the latest in a long series of CIA blunders. Over the past half century, U.S. presidents have accepted the poor performance of the CIA, presumably because the agency represents a clandestine and relatively inexpensive instrument of American foreign policy. President Dwight Eisenhower employed the CIA in a series of covert actions in Guatemala, Iran, and Cuba that contributed to instability in these countries and complicated U.S. bilateral relations in the Caribbean and Southwest Asia. Subsequent covert operations in Indonesia, Congo, Angola, and Chile followed a similar pattern. In the 1980s, CIA Director William Casey politicized the intelligence analysis of the CIA and orchestrated the Iran-contra scheme that eventually embarrassed the Reagan administration. Deputy Director Robert Gates failed to receive confirmation as CIA director in 1987 because the Senate Select Committee on Intelligence did not believe his denials of knowledge of the Iran-contra affair. Casey and Gates were directly responsible for the CIA's poor analytical record in dealing with Soviet issues throughout the 1980s, from the failure to foresee the Soviet collapse to the revelation that CIA clandestine officer Aldrich Ames had been a Soviet spy for nearly a decade— the greatest intelligence failure in the history of the agency until the terrorist attacks in 2001.

The performance of the intelligence community did not improve in the 1990s. When the CIA missed India's underground nuclear testing in 1998, Tenet stated, "We didn't have a clue."[138] This failure to monitor Indian testing and Tenet's inexplicable testimony that the CIA could not guarantee verification of the treaty led to the Senate's unwillingness to ratify the Comprehensive Test Ban Treaty. The CIA also failed to anticipate the third-stage capability of North Korea's Taepodong missile, which was tested in August 1998, leading to bipartisan calls in the United States for more funding for national missile defense and Japanese suspension of talks to establish diplomatic relations with North Korea.[199] Since 1998, CIA analysis of Third World missile programs has taken on a worst-case flavor, exaggerating the national security threat to the United States and politicizing the intelligence data in the process.

The CIA has been particularly weak on the terrorism issue. In 1986, Casey and Gates created the conceptually flawed Counter-Terrorism Center (CTC). They believed that the Soviet Union was responsible for every act of international terrorism (it wasn't), that intelligence analysts and secret agents should work together in one office (they shouldn't), and that the CIA and other intelligence agencies would share sensitive information (they didn't). The CIA and FBI provided no warning of terrorist attacks on the World Trade Center in 1993, U.S. military barracks in Saudi Arabia in 1996, U.S. embassies in East Africa in 1998, and the USS *Cole* in 2000. Presumably there were intelligence successes during this period that may have prevented other acts of terrorism. Nevertheless, the CTC never understood the connection between Ramzi Ahmed Yousef, the coordinator of the 1993 World Trade Center attack, and the al-Qaeda organization until it was too late. And the CTC expected an attack abroad, not at home.

The September 11 attack exposed the inability of analysts and agents to perform strategic analysis, challenge flawed assumptions, and share sensitive secrets. No agency in the intelligence community could imagine a terrorist operation conducted inside the United States, using commercial airplanes as weapons, although al-Qaeda had planned such operations in the mid-1990s in Europe and Asia. The CIA was tracking al-Qaeda operatives but never placed them on the immigration service watch list; the FBI failed to track Arab men attending flight schools who were behaving in a suspicious fashion. Nevertheless, the Congressional Research Service and University of Pennsylvania professor of political science Stephen Gale did anticipate hijacking of commercial aircraft and warned both the CIA and the Department of Transportation.[140]

Since September 11, the Bush administration's global policy of unilateralism has involved the CIA in controversial covert operations, including political assassinations, despite the ban since 1975 on such actions by presidential executive order. U.S. unilateralism and fear of the CIA are major components of the anti-Americanism that is intensifying in Europe, the Middle East, and Southwest Asia. The current CIA director, George Tenet, is serving the policy interests of the Bush administration in other ways as well, resorting to worst-case analysis to describe the threats that confront the United States in order to justify the deployment of a national missile defense and the U.S. withdrawal from the Anti-Ballistic Missile Treaty, a cornerstone of U.S. arms control policy since 1972. Without new data, CIA analysts have begun asserting that Iran, Iraq, and North Korea are moving closer to a nuclear capability that would threaten the United States. The administration's pressure on the CIA to produce intelligence data to justify a war against Iraq will lead to greater politicization of intelligence, and the emphasis on preemptive attack will lead to dubious demands on the CIA to produce intelligence justification for warfare. Tenet's unprecedented diplomatic role in the Middle East peace process revives the suspicion that a CIA director has put the nation's strategic intelligence at the service of a political agenda. His intense involvement with both Palestinian and Israeli security forces places him at the center of the policy process in the Middle East and compromises the collection of unbiased intelligence.

STRUCTURAL FLAWS

One reason for the consistent failures of the intelligence community is the organizational overload at both the CIA and FBI. The CIA has an operational mission to collect human intelligence and analyze and publish national intelligence estimates. It is also responsible for covert action. The agency cannot perform both missions well. The FBI also suffers from a bipolar mission. Its traditional law enforcement mission involves reacting to crimes that have already occurred. Its counterterrorism mission, by contrast, requires a proactive role—ferreting out threats to national security before they occur. Walter Lippmann reminded us seventy years ago that it is essential to "separate as absolutely as it is possible to do so the staff which executes from the staff which investigates."[141]

Turf issues abound. The protection of "sources and methods" has been an obstacle to information sharing, with the CIA and the FBI having a long history of poor communication. As critical, intelligence agencies and the Pentagon often lock horns. The director of central intelligence (DCI) is responsible for foreign intelligence but lacks control and authority over 90 percent of the intelligence community, including the National Security Agency (NSA), the National Imagery and Mapping Agency (NIMA), and the National Reconnaissance Office (NRO), which are staffed and funded by the Department of Defense. The priorities of the DCI and those of the Pentagon are quite different. Previous DCIs, particularly Gates and John Deutch, harmed the CIA by de-emphasizing strategic intelligence for policy makers and catering instead to the tactical demands of the

Pentagon. The CIA produced fewer intelligence assessments that dealt with strategic matters and emphasized instead intelligence support for the war fighter. Gates ended CIA analysis on key order-of-battle issues in order to avoid tendentious analytical struggles with the Pentagon; Deutch's creation of NIMA at the Department of Defense enabled the Pentagon to be the sole interpreter of satellite photography. The Pentagon uses imagery analysis to justify the defense budget, to gauge the likelihood of military conflict around the world, and to verify arms control agreements. In creating NIMA, Deutch abolished the CIA's Office of Imagery Analysis and the joint Department of Defense–CIA National Photographic Interpretation Center, which often challenged the analytical views of the Pentagon. Worst of all, the Bush administration has referred to a "marriage" between the Pentagon and the CIA, which suggests that intelligence continues to be subordinated to Pentagon priorities. The CIA's worst-case analysis is being used to justify the highest peacetime increases in defense spending since the record-level hikes during the Reagan administration.

The CIA's second major mission, covert action, remains a dangerously unregulated activity. There are no political and ethical guidelines delineating when to engage in covert action, and previous covert actions have harmed U.S. strategic interests, placing on the CIA payroll such criminals as Panama's General Manuel Noriega, Guatemala's Colonel Julio Alpirez, Peru's intelligence chief Vladimiro Montesinos, and Chile's General Manuel Contreras. Although President Bush, like every other president since Gerald Ford, has signed an executive order banning political assassination, exceptions have been made in the covert pursuit of Iraqi President Saddam Hussein and former Afghanistan Prime Minister Gulbuddin Hekmatyar—both of whom also, ironically, received CIA assistance in the

1980s. In November 2002, the CIA killed six al-Qaeda operatives in Yemen, an action immediately condemned by Amnesty International as a violation of international law prohibiting summary executions.

In 1998, the United States and the CIA used the cover of the UN and the UN Special Commission (UNSCOM) to conduct a secret operation to spy on Iraqi military communications as part of a covert action to topple Saddam Hussein. Neither the UN nor UNSCOM had authorized the U.S. surveillance, which Saddam Hussein cited as justification for expelling the UN monitors. As a result, the United States and the UN lost its most successful program to monitor and verify Iraq's nuclear, chemical, and biological programs, compromising the credibility of multilateral inspection of weapons of mass destruction. In that same year, the CIA produced spurious intelligence data to justify the U.S. bombing of a pharmaceutical plant in the Sudan, one of the few countries willing to help the Clinton administration arrest Osama bin Laden.[142]

Finally, a comparison of the CIA and the State Department reveals skewed U.S. priorities. Today, the CIA has approximately sixteen thousand employees, more than four times the number at the State Department, and the intelligence community budget is ten times that of the State Department. As a result of cutbacks, the State Department has had to close important posts in South America, the Balkans, Southwest Asia, and Africa, and has had to post political amateurs with deep pockets to key ambassadorships. It is no wonder that the role of the State Department has significantly diminished in such key functional areas as arms control and disarmament and such key regional areas as the Middle East and South Asia. The CIA, meanwhile, doesn't need so many resources. One of the CIA's first directors, Allen Dulles, emphasized that "the bulk of intelligence can be obtained through overt channels" and that if the agency got to be a "great big octopus it would not function well."[143]

WHAT IS TO BE DONE?

What the CIA and the intelligence community should be, what it should do, and what it should prepare to do is less clear now than at any time since the beginning of the Cold War. Throughout the Cold War, the need to count and characterize Soviet weapons systems and the search for indications of surprise attack focused the efforts of the CIA. These goals disappeared with the collapse of the Berlin Wall in 1989 and the dissolution of the Soviet Union in 1991. Major steps must be taken to design an intelligence infrastructure to deal with terrorism, the major security threat in the twenty-first century. The ongoing contentious debate over the proposed new Department of Homeland Security masks the far greater need to reform the intelligence community. Such reforms include demilitarizing the intelligence community, resolution of key turf issues, and reform of covert operations.

Retired general Brent Scowcroft has conducted a comprehensive review of the intelligence community for President Bush and favors transferring budgetary and collection authority from the Pentagon to a new office that reports directly to the DCI.[144] These agencies include NSA, which conducts worldwide electronic eavesdropping; NRO, which designs spy satellites; and NIMA, which analyzes satellite pictures and data and produces maps.[145] Secretary of Defense Donald Rumsfeld opposes this transfer and has created a new position of undersecretary of defense for intelligence to preempt such reform. Congressional approval of this new position would preserve the status quo and close the narrow window of opportunity for more extensive reform proposals under consideration by the joint intelligence committees of the House and Senate.

It is crucial that the CIA strengthen links across the intelligence community in order to share intelligence. Unfortunately, the agency places too much emphasis on the compartmentalization of intelligence and the "need to know," which are obstacles to intelligence sharing. The failures at Pearl Harbor in 1941 and the terrorist attacks in 2001 could have been prevented with genuine sharing of sensitive intelligence information. But this information tends to move vertically within each of the thirteen intelligence agencies instead of horizontally across them. The FBI and the CIA have never been effective in sharing information with each other or with such key agencies as the Immigration and Naturalization Service, the Federal Aviation Agency, the Border Guards, and the Coast Guard, which will be on the front lines in the war against terrorism. There is no guarantee that the CIA and FBI will share raw reporting on terrorism with the new Office of Homeland Security.

To minimize the politicization of intelligence work, covert operations and intelligence gathering should be separated. The CIA's directorate of operations is responsible for clandestine activities. Relying on secrecy, hierarchy, and the strict enforcement of information on a need-to-know basis, it is involved in the policy-making process. The directorate of intelligence, on the other hand, helps set the context for people who formulate policy, but it should not be involved in the making of policy. The FBI should likewise be split into two agencies, with a domestic counterterrorism service reporting directly to the director of central intelligence.

The Bush administration and Congress have responded in classic bureaucratic fashion to the September 11 failure, throwing lots of money at the problem to find a solution.

The defense budget for 2003 will be close to $400 billion, an increase of nearly 30 percent since 2000. The intelligence budget will increase by 20 percent in 2003, climbing to more than $35 billion. The defense budget protects the current force structure and ongoing weapons modernization programs, and assigns top priority to deploying a national missile defense. Most of the intelligence budget pays for collection resources—including a profusion of electronic data and images from planes, ships, ground stations, and satellites, along with clandestine human intelligence collection. These increases have little to do with countering terrorism and are reminiscent of President Dwight Eisenhower's warning against the military-industrial complex in 1961.

The intelligence community, particularly the CIA, faces a situation comparable to that of fifty-five years ago, when President Harry S. Truman created the CIA and the National Security Council. As in 1947–48, the international environment has now been recast, the threats have been altered, and as a result the institutions created to fight the Cold War must be redesigned. If steps are not taken to improve the intelligence community, we can certainly expect more terrorist operations against the United States.

CULTURE
by Noy Thrupkaew

IOWA FARMER BOB OSBORNE is a key U.S. agent in the war on terrorism. The public relations part of it, that is.

A *Good Morning Egypt* crew paid Osborne a visit at his Shellsburg, Iowa, dairy farm in early 2002. Anchor Shereen el Wakeel told her viewers, "I wanted to address some of the stereotypes we have of Americans from TV and movies—people in fancy clothes, girls in tight pants," and robust Bob

Osborne and his overalls seemed just the right counterimage.[146]

The *Good Morning Egypt* show was the result of a U.S. government–funded exchange program for Arab and Arab-American journalists—just one of the latest tactics in the U.S. public diplomacy campaign to win support for its war on terrorism.

Meanwhile, a few weeks after the Egyptian show aired in May 2002, a committee of Hollywood executives called "Hollywood 9/11" released their first U.S. contribution to the war effort. From Memorial Day to the Fourth of July and again on the one-year anniversary of September 11, three public service announcements (PSAs) promoting volunteerism and the Citizen Corps—the administration's volunteer program to mobilize local communities' ability to respond to and prevent threats of terrorism—played across TV and theater screens.

One highly controversial component of the Citizen Corps put an ominous spin on the phrase "public service." First proposed in January 2002, Operation TIPS would have turned workers into government spies. In its pilot stage, Operation TIPS planned to recruit a million people, including letter carriers, utility workers, train conductors, and truckers "in a unique position to serve as extra eyes and ears for law enforcement."[147] Informants were to report to a government hotline any unusual activities they might observe during their daily routines. The U.S. Postal Service refused to participate in the operation, and conservative congressional leader Dick Armey ultimately excised the program from the Homeland Security bill.[148]

As these efforts testify, the U.S. government has waged a war of words as much as a war of weapons in its recent campaign against terrorism. Overseas, the Bush administration launched an all-out public relations offensive, particularly in the Middle East and the rest of the Muslim world. On the home front, in contrast, it has worked to keep things quiet by tightly controlling press access to information, stoppering government leaks, and stoking patriotic sentiment through PSAs, commercials, and the story lines of TV dramas and reality-based series.

This cultural "hearts and minds" campaign is the Bush administration's attempt at harnessing "soft power"—or, as Joseph Nye explains, "getting people to want what you want."[149] While "hard power" is often enforced through military action, "soft power" is the carrot side of the carrot-and-stick technique of ensuring cooperation; by presenting itself as an enviably open, prosperous, and democratic society, a country can convince others to emulate it or go along with its policies. The U.S. government has a powerful soft power tool at its disposal—American culture and the many enticing forms in which it appears abroad: Hollywood, American products, images of comfort and wealth. Although American culture may be reviled by conservatives, religious fundamentalists, and the French, it is strongly embraced even in the Middle East by moderates and younger people.

Whatever the inherent allure of American culture, the Bush administration's efforts to yoke its messages to radio channels, movies, and pamphlets have been largely ineffective. Behind the soft power strategies, distinctly "un-American" hard power problems of censorship, deception, undemocratic information control, and one-sided "cultural exchange" loom large. At home, tight media controls and the curtailing of civil liberties belie the PR campaign's rhetoric of "freedom and democracy." And as long as U.S. policy is perceived as deviating from the values the Bush administration touts, skeptics will not likely be swayed by the leaflets, commercials, broadcasts, or PSAs the government is spending millions to produce.

The person behind much of the overseas public diplomacy effort was Charlotte Beers. A Madison Avenue advertising star with no diplomacy experience, Beers might seem an unlikely choice for a top State Department official. But as Colin Powell explained, "I wanted one of the world's greatest advertising experts, because what are we doing? We're selling. We're selling a product. That product we are selling is democracy. It's the free enterprise system, the American value system."[150]

Beers's efforts as undersecretary of state for public diplomacy and public affairs were complemented at home by the work of the White House "war room." The Bush administration's top communications directors met every morning in the Old Executive Office Building to coordinate their messages for the domestic audience. Right after the attacks, the war room's burden seemed lighter than that of Beers. After September 11, the American public seemed sold on Powell's "American value system." Stars and stripes blazed from miniskirts and flip-flops, and posters of the flag sported the defiant slogan: "These colors don't run." Recording artists released covers of the anthem; an "American Spirit" channel appeared on Internet radio station Spinner.

Hollywood also responded to the attacks, performing a sort of self-censorship by shelving content that would have been standard fare before September 11. One example is the fate of Arnold Schwarzenegger's *Collateral Damage*, about a man seeking revenge for the terrorism-related deaths of his family. Originally slated for release in October, the movie was delayed for months. Other films excised all references to the twin towers. Ben Stiller's *Zoolander*, for example, digitally erased the buildings from the New York skyline.

Some Hollywood executives are also taking a more proactive role, meeting with White House officials to help determine how Tinseltown can best assist in the war on terrorism. Immediately after the attacks, Hollywood writers flocked to "brainstorming sessions" attended by Pentagon officials and put on by the Institute for Creative Technologies, a video training research institution funded by the Army. The writers' mission: to guess at what the terrorists might do next. In November, Hollywood bigwigs filed into the posh Beverly Peninsula Hotel to meet with White House senior adviser Karl Rove, who itemized the Bush message: the war is on terrorism, not Islam; Americans must embrace national service; Americans should support the forces overseas; the global conflict requires a global response; the war is a fight against evil; American children should feel reassured and safe; and the war would be fueled not by propaganda but by a clear and accurate narrative. Although film and TV "content were not on the table," according to Jack Valenti, the head of the Motion Picture Association of America, Karl Rove and the White House clearly wanted their message plugged into Hollywood productions.[151]

Not much has come of "Hollywood 9/11." The group's most significant achievements are the coordination of movie shipments to the troops overseas and the production of the PSAs. The most ambitious plans—filming PSAs to run internationally—have been the least successful; early talks to cast Muhammad Ali in a PSA for Muslim audiences ultimately fell through. Four PSAs finally debuted in October 2002 in Indonesia and other countries with large Muslim populations, but many Indonesian viewers dismissed them as little more than propaganda.[152]

Despite the "no content" pledge of the Hollywood 9/11 summit, the Pentagon has managed to insinuate itself into the planning of a few television scripts and dramas. The most visible examples of the Pentagon's involvement have occurred in episodes of *JAG* and *The West Wing*, and in the development of new reality-based series that focus on the military. In the CBS military show *JAG*, the show's producers staged a military tribunal in one episode—with an al-Qaeda member on trial. The show has long enjoyed a close relationship with the Pentagon in order to secure authentic locations and props. According to one Pentagon official, "We offer our assistance when we think it is in the best interest of the Department of Defense and our people, and it's up to the production company to accept it. If they go on and say, 'Thanks but no thanks, we won't make our character be what you stand for,' we are less inclined to support them."[153]

Jerry Bruckheimer, producer of hyperpatriotic, testosterone-filled blockbusters such as *Top Gun, Pearl Harbor*, and *Black Hawk Down*, teamed up with *Cops* producer Bertram van Munster to develop a fall 2002 ABC reality series that followed soldiers in Afghanistan. VH1 has its own military reality show *Military Diaries*, that features the video diaries of soldiers edited into thirteen thirty-minute episodes.

CONTROLLING THE MESSAGE

According to New York's *Sunday Tribune*, "Most television networks have…taken their orders directly from the Pentagon" and enjoyed a good deal of access to military installations as a result.[154] Journalists, on the other hand, have found themselves standing out in the cold. CBS anchor Dan Rather told the *New York Times*, "Somebody's got to question whether it's a good idea to limit independent reporting on the battlefield and access of journalists to U.S. military personnel and then conspire with Hollywood."[155] The administration has maintained a tight hold on military information, surprising even seasoned spokespeople of other conflicts. Barry Zorthian, chief spokesman for the

American campaign in Vietnam from 1964 to 1968, told the *New York Times* that the flow of information in this conflict is "much tighter than Vietnam."[156]

Commentators and editorial writers who disagreed with the administration came under fire. The *Daily Courier* in Oregon sacked a columnist who criticized Bush for his less-than-rapid return to the capital following the attacks. The *Texas City Sun* issued an apology for a column written by a city editor entitled "Bush Failed to Lead the U.S." and fired the editor. *Washington Post* columnist Mary McGrory's column criticizing the president's action following the attacks drew more angry letters from readers than any other column in her forty-year career.[157]

Perhaps the most public blowout took place after Bill Maher, host of the ABC-TV show *Politically Incorrect,* said, "We have been the cowards, lobbing cruise missiles from two thousand miles away. That's cowardly. Staying in the airplane when it hits the building, say what you want about it, is not cowardly."[158] Stations across the country dropped or suspended Maher's show, even as Maher scrambled to apologize for his remarks. At the White House, Press Secretary Ari Fleischer warned Americans that "they need to watch what they say, watch what they do. This is not a time for remarks like that. There never is."[159] Although *Politically Incorrect* was canceled in May 2002, the network insisted that Maher's comments about September 11 had nothing to do with the decision. Maher had another take on the matter. "To them, *Politically Incorrect* was just, ooh, a cool title," he said of the network. "I don't think they really got it, that I really was politically incorrect."[160]

Even more politically incorrect was the Pentagon's short-lived Office of Strategic Information. In February 2002, Secretary of Defense Donald Rumsfeld announced the closing of the Pentagon's controversial office only seven days after allegations surfaced that the office's mandate may have included purposefully deceiving foreign media and running covert operations characterized by one Pentagon official as the "blackest of black programs."[161] Rumsfeld vehemently denied that the office had ever been involved in spreading misinformation, or would have done so. "I guess notwithstanding the fact that much of the thrust of the criticism and the cartoons and the editorial has been off the mark," Rumsfeld said in a February 2002 news briefing, "the office has clearly been so damaged that...it's pretty clear to me that it could not function effectively."[162]

Despite Rumsfeld's protestations to the contrary, shortly before the United States launched its bombing initiative in Afghanistan, an unidentified military officer told the *Washington Post*, "This is the most information-intensive war you can imagine.... We're going to lie about things."[163] And when the *New York Times* inquired about closed-door meetings Charlotte Beers was holding for foreign journalists, the State Department's Deputy Director of Media Price Floyd explained, "We can't give out our propaganda to our own people."[164]

INEFFECTUAL EXPORTS

What has the State Department been "giving out" overseas? Among other actions, Beers increased funding to cultural exchanges, produced a Web site (www.state.gov/r/) and a pamphlet on terrorism and September 11, and launched a popular Arabic radio station. A satellite television station is also in the works.

Although Beers made some headway, before resigning in March 2003 citing health reasons, her major projects seem largely ineffective. Radio Sawa, perhaps her most popular measure, began broadcasting in spring 2002 on a

Even more dramatic has been the escalation of U.S. threats against Iraq, including a willingness to invade the country and install a new government. One justification for intervention has been alleged Iraqi support of terrorism. Various administration charges of links between the Iraqi government and the al-Qaeda network have, upon independent investigation, proven groundless.

It is unlikely that the decidedly secular Baathist regime—which has savagely suppressed Islamists within Iraq—would maintain close links with bin Laden and his followers. According to Prince Turki bin Faisal, former Saudi intelligence chief, bin Laden views Saddam Hussein "as an apostate, an infidel or someone who is not worthy of being a fellow Muslim," and offered in 1990 to recruit thousands of mujahedin fighters to drive Iraqi occupation forces out of Kuwait.[174] Iraq's past terrorist links have largely been limited to such secular organizations as the defunct Palestinian group led by the late Abu Nidal. At the height of Iraq's support of Abu Nidal, in the early 1980s, the United States dropped Iraq from its terrorism list in order to support Iraq's war effort against Iran. Only after its invasion of Kuwait was Iraq returned to the list despite a lack of evidence of increased ties to terrorism. A recent CIA report indicates that the Iraqis have been consciously avoiding any actions against the United States or its facilities abroad,[175] and the State Department's own survey in 2001 found virtually no current Iraqi links to international terrorism.[176]

With the terrorism link unproven, the Bush administration tried to justify an invasion on the grounds that the Iraqi government might be developing weapons of mass destruction. However, no one in the Bush administration has been able to present any evidence that Iraq actually developed such weapons or that it has been able to replenish its missiles and other delivery systems, virtually all of which were accounted for and destroyed by UN inspectors. Former chief UN weapons inspector Scott Ritter, on his visit to Iraq in September 2002, reiterated his contention that the country is incapable of developing any weapons of mass destruction with offensive capability.[177] Similarly, there has been no credible scenario put forward as to why the Iraqis might be inclined to launch what would inevitably be a suicidal first strike against the United States or its allies. Iraq's previous use of chemical weapons, done with the knowledge that the United States and other major powers would look the other way, was restricted to Kurdish civilians who could not strike back and Iranian soldiers who had no powerful allies. Nor has Saddam Hussein, who practices a highly centralized style of leadership, shown any indication of passing on weapons of mass destruction to terrorists he would have no guarantee of controlling. Still, the administration argues that any regime that poses even a *potential* threat to the United States should be replaced with one more compliant with U.S. interests, an unprecedented expansion of the official American position on what justifies the use of force.

Furthermore, the Bush administration has continued the Clinton policy that weapons of mass destruction are an acceptable part of the arsenals of the United States and such regional allies as Israel and Pakistan, but not so for Iraq. In a clear shift from the Clinton administration, however, the Bush administration refused to support the return of weapons inspectors and their enhanced mandate for rigorous inspections, launching an invasion of Iraq in March 2003 despite pleas from the chief inspectors and the UN Secretary General to give them time to complete their mission.

To support a U.S. assault on Baghdad, the Bush administration has also attempted to bring the weak and disparate Iraqi opposition groups together to form a provisional government and to launch an armed insurgency, but with little success. Meanwhile, the Arab states that supported the United States in the 1991 Gulf War were reluctant to get behind a U.S. invasion. Most European governments, though open to the use of force under certain conditions, have also expressed their firm opposition to a unilateral U.S. invasion.

PRESSURING PALESTINE

In Israel, Ariel Sharon, the far–right-wing general implicated in a series of war crimes against Palestinian civilians, was elected prime minister just weeks after President Bush assumed office in 2001. Sharon played a key role in precipitating the outbreak of the second intifada in September 2000 when, as talks between Israel and Palestine broke down at Camp David, he made a provocative trip to a religious site claimed by both Jews and Muslims in Israeli-occupied East Jerusalem. On taking office, Sharon refused to reenter peace negotiations with the Palestinians, and the repression in the occupied territories increased dramatically.

Despite State Department and CIA analyses criticizing Sharon's ongoing provocations and overreactions, Bush has focused almost exclusively on Palestinian terrorism as the cause of the crisis, using the same basic rhetoric as Sharon.[178] Under Bush, Defense Department officials have unprecedented clout in the formulation of U.S. policy toward the conflict, which had previously been largely under the purview of the State Department. As a result, hard-line Pentagon officials who view the conflict strictly in security terms—Secretary of Defense Donald Rumsfeld, Deputy Secretary of Defense Paul Wolfowitz, and Undersecretary of Defense Douglas Feith—have marginalized the more pragmatic conservatives, such as Secretary of

State Colin Powell, who see the conflict more in political terms. Feith and Wolfowitz have long been on record opposing the peace process and have advocated continued Israeli occupation of the West Bank and Gaza Strip.[179] These hawkish voices have been augmented significantly by a coalition of Democrats and right-wing Republicans in Congress who also support an expansionist Israel and oppose Israeli moderates calling for an end to Israeli occupation of Palestinian lands in exchange for security guarantees.[180] The struggle in the occupied territories, in the eyes of the Bush administration and both parties in Congress, is not a matter of the military occupation of one country by another, but the suppression of terrorism. Without U.S. pressure, the Israelis have refused to lift their siege of Palestinian towns and cities or end the border closures. Not surprisingly, the violence has continued.

At the multilateral level, the United States has blocked the UN from authorizing a multinational peacekeeping force, human rights monitors, or even an inspection team to investigate an alleged massacre by Israeli occupation forces at a Palestinian refugee camp. The United States scuttled a series of proposed UN resolutions by European nations by threatening to veto anything that used the term "siege" to refer to Israeli occupation forces surrounding and shelling Palestinian towns, or that mentioned Israel's illegal settlements, the Geneva Conventions, international law, or the principle of land-for-peace. In December 2001, the United States vetoed a UN Security Council resolution strongly condemning Palestinian terrorism because it also criticized Israeli policies of assassinating Palestinian dissidents and imposing collective punishment on civilian populations. In December 2002, the United States vetoed a measure criticizing Israel's slaying of UN humanitarian workers and the destruction of a food warehouse belonging to a UN development agency. In each of these cases, the United States was the only dissenter within the fifteen-member world body.

In June 2002, in the face of a new wave of terrorist attacks by Palestinian extremists inside Israel and the reconquest of Palestinian cities by Israeli forces, President Bush gave a major policy speech in the White House Rose Garden on Israel and Palestine. The president described what steps the United States would insist were necessary to propel the peace process forward. After more than thirty years of rejecting the international consensus, President Bush made the most explicit statement by an American president to date affirming that peace requires the establishment of a Palestinian state alongside a secure Israel. However, his speech focused upon the idea that while Israel's right to exist is a given, Palestine's right to exist—even as a ministate on the West Bank and Gaza Strip—is conditional. Perhaps the most striking element of the speech was his assertion that U.S. support for Palestinian statehood was predicated on major internal reforms by the Palestinian Authority. "Peace requires a new and different Palestinian leadership," Bush insisted, "so that a Palestinian state can be born."[181] Furthermore, the Bush administration's concept of a Palestinian "state" apparently falls far short of a viable Palestinian nation, but it would look more like the infamous Bantustans of apartheid South Africa, tiny noncontiguous parcels of land surrounded by Israeli settlements and military outposts.

The irony is that whatever the many faults of Yasir Arafat and the Palestinian Authority, the Palestinian negotiating position on the outstanding issues in the peace talks—regarding Jerusalem, the rights of refugees, Israeli withdrawal from occupied territory, and the Jewish settlements—is far more consistent with international law and UN Security Council resolutions than that of the Israelis. Despite that, President Bush has insisted that Palestinians, not Israelis, need new leadership in order for the peace process to move forward. Similarly, President Bush has focused primarily on Palestinian violence against Israeli civilians, although Israeli occupation forces have killed far more Palestinian civilians than Palestinian terrorists have killed Israeli civilians.

The Bush administration has also refused to promote the March 2002 peace plan of Saudi Prince Abdullah. Endorsed by the Palestinian Authority and every single Arab government, the plan offers Israel security guarantees and full normal relations in return for withdrawal from the occupied territories seized in the 1967 war—essentially a reiteration of UN Security Council Resolutions 242 and 338, which most previous U.S. administrations had declared to be the basis for Arab-Israeli peace.

BUILDING REAL SECURITY

Even though the stakes are higher than ever, the Bush administration appears to be continuing the policy of previous administrations of allowing ideological and economic imperatives to take precedence over the country's real security interests.

For example, there is increasing evidence that some leading segments of Saudi society, including members of the Saudi royal family, support terrorism. Much of the financing for al-Qaeda comes from this U.S. ally, and fifteen of the nineteen hijackers were Saudi citizens. Instead of targeting Saudi Arabia, however, the war on terrorism has included countries with no apparent links to al-Qaeda, such as Iran, Iraq, Syria, and Palestine. Similarly, the Bush administration continues to support a fundamentalist and authoritarian regime in Saudi Arabia while refusing to support the Palestinians' right to statehood until they create a demo-

Top Arms Recipients in the Middle East: 1998–2001		
Country	U.S. Deliveries	Total Receipts
Saudi Arabia	$12.8	$29.3
Israel	$3.8	$4.8
Egypt	$3.1	$3.5
Kuwait	$1.5	$2.4

Note: Figures in current $U.S. billions

Source: Richard F. Grimmett, *Conventional Arms Transfers to Developing Nations* (Washington, DC: Congressional Research Service, August 6, 2002), p. 37.

cratic political system based upon "tolerance and liberty."[182] The Saudi regime's close ties to American oil interests have made it difficult for successive administrations to challenge the country's repressive theocratic rule and ties to Islamic extremists. Ironically, the belated emergence of anti-Saudi rumblings in Washington in the summer and fall of 2002 appears to have come from those angered not at the government's domestic repression or ties to terrorists, but at its initiatives to resolve the Israeli-Palestinian conflict and avert a war against Iraq.

U.S. military presence in Saudi Arabia led Osama bin Laden to shift from an American ally in the 1980s to its most prominent nemesis and has given Saddam Hussein as well as hard-line elements in Iran an excuse to continue their hostility and militancy. Given the clear military superiority of the six allied Arab monarchies of the Gulf Cooperation Council (GCC) relative to both Iran and Iraq, a withdrawal of American forces from the region would actually improve America's security interests without harming the security needs of allied regimes. Indeed, it would likely contribute to tentative efforts to establish a regional security regime by the six GCC states, Iraq, and Iran, an effort the United States should support. This could be expanded to include serious disarmament efforts for the whole region, including the prohibition of weapons of mass destruction not just by Iraq and Iran, but by all countries of the Middle East.

Regarding Israel and Palestine, the United States should end its support for Ariel Sharon's occupation policies and join the European Union, the Arab League, and virtually the entire international community in supporting the formula of land for peace: the total withdrawal of Israeli occupation forces and settlers from the West Bank and Gaza Strip, the establishment of a viable Palestinian state alongside Israel, a shared Jerusalem, and a just settlement of the refugee problem in return for strict security guarantees for Israel. This could even include a formal military alliance between the United States and Israel to protect the legitimate security interests of the Jewish state once Israel withdraws from the territories captured in the 1967 war.

The United States became the target of terrorists not because of the country's freedom and democracy, as President Bush claims, but because U.S. Middle East policy has had nothing to do with freedom and democracy. A policy based more on support for democracy, international law, arms control, and sustainable development will make American interests far safer than the current policy based on punitive sanctions, invasion, arms exports, and support for repression and economic policies that primarily benefit wealthy elites. The shift to the right in U.S. Middle East policy actually began when the Clinton administration came to office. However, the events of September 11, 2001, made it politically possible for the United States to move in an even more extreme direction. Most prominent Democrats in Congress, including traditional skeptics of U.S. foreign policy, were supportive of this rightward drift during the Clinton administration out of party loyalty and have remained largely supportive of Bush's Middle East policy as well out of fear of being labeled "soft on terrorism." It is very unlikely, then, that there will be a shift in U.S. Middle East policy unless a popular movement develops within the United States to force such a change.

AFRICA
by Martha Honey

IT WAS A POWERFULLY symbolic gift, coming as it did from one of the world's poorer countries to the world's richest. In June 2002, a Maasai village in Kenya presented its most precious resource, fifteen head of cattle, to the United States as an expression of solidarity for the tragedy of September 11. "To the people of America, we give these cows to help you," read banners at the ceremonial handover of the cattle from Maasai elders to the U.S. ambassador.[183] The gift was all the more poignant since the U.S. government still has not compensated the families of the Kenyan victims of terrorism who died in al-Qaeda's1998 bombing of the U.S. embassy in Nairobi.[184]

This was the latest of a long string of gestures of sympathy from different parts of Africa. Immediately after September 11, the Organization of African Union (OAU, since renamed African Union) expressed its "full solidarity" and "deepest condolence," and African leaders, even those usually at odds with the United States, offered their support. Libya's Muammar Qaddafi sent condolences for the "horrific" attacks and offered to donate his blood to the U.S. victims. Sudan, which once housed Osama bin Laden, offered cooperation in tracking al-Qaeda terrorists. Ethiopia, Djibouti, Nigeria, and Kenya, among others, shut down or froze suspected terrorist financial networks operating in their countries, while once-leftist Eritrea offered the United States use of its territory and port as a military base to fight terrorism.[185] Nigeria, home of Africa's largest Muslim population, drafted antiterrorist legislation, while South Africa offered its support for U.S.-led diplomatic efforts to fight terrorism. And during an African summit in Dakar in October 2001, Senegalese president Abdoulaye Wade proposed an African Pact Against Terrorism and created a regional counterterrorism intelligence center, with U.S. assistance.[186]

At the same time, several African governments opportunistically hitched their own counterinsurgency campaigns to Washington's global war on terrorism. In Africa's longest-running civil war, the Sudanese government labeled Christian and animist separatists as terrorists; Eritrean president Isaias Afewerki, a liberator turned increasingly dictatorial, used the post–September 11 period to crack down on dissent; and Zimbabwean leader Robert Mugabe termed his largely nonviolent political opponents "terrorists."[187] Close U.S. allies Daniel arap Moi in Kenya (voted out of office in December 2002) and Olusegun Obasanjo in Nigeria tried to bolster their own hold on power by forging closer ties with the U.S. military.

But in this mix of genuine sympathy and political opportunism, many Africans were wary, as well, of being too closely associated with Washington's war on terrorism. African states feared repercussions both from and on their own Muslim populations. Roughly 40 percent of Africans are Muslims with large concentrations in North Africa, the East African coast, and West African countries such as Nigeria and Senegal.[188] In the days after September 11, there were scattered street celebrations in Muslim strongholds in northern Nigeria and Somalia, and subsequent anti-American protests in Sudan, South Africa, and Kenya. African leaders also feared that the United States would pursue its war on terrorism throughout the continent. By January 2002, as U.S. military attacks in Afghanistan wound down, the United States turned its sights on a handful of countries suspected of harboring al-Qaeda terrorists, including Libya, Egypt, Sudan, and Somalia. "These governments are afraid they might be the next U.S. target, and are therefore clearly keen to show they are cooperating in the war against terrorism," commented a diplomat stationed in Nairobi.[189]

Somalia, with its lack of a stable central government, was most clearly in Washington's crosshairs. Its transitional government hastily declared bin Laden persona non grata and arrested eight Iraqis and a Palestinian as terrorist suspects. The detentions were largely symbolic; as one U.S. government adviser noted, those detained were probably "a few poor Iraqi migrants looking for cooking jobs in Mogadishu."[190] Indeed, the United States, while continuing to deny Somalia diplomatic recognition, took extremely crippling measures against this impoverished country with only rudimentary state functions. Contending that it may have ties to al-Qaeda, the United States branded as "terrorist" the indigenous group al-Itihad al-Islami (AIAI), which is fighting for an Islamic state.[191] Most damaging, the United States closed down al-Barakat, Somalia's biggest employer and largest remittance bank-cum-telephone service, thereby cutting off both communications and $500 million a year sent home by Somali expatriates. The United States also severed Somalia's Internet links, monitored international air flights, and sent naval forces to barricade the coast.[192] As in Afghanistan, the United States sought the use of local and regional surrogate forces. For instance, the Somali Restoration and Reconciliation Council (SRRC), an Ethiopian-backed group, helped the United States identify possible terrorist bases.[193] The leader of SRRC is the son of

Mohammed Aidid, the Somali clan leader that U.S. Special Forces were pursuing so unsuccessfully in the early 1990s. September 11 has created many strange bedfellows, but this Somalia campaign netted no significant al-Qaeda operatives.

TERRORISM IN AFRICA

Africa, of course, has not been untouched by terrorism, some homegrown, some linked to international networks. As early as 1990, Egyptian President Hosni Mubarak began warning that international terrorism represented a bigger danger than war. In 1995, Islamic fundamentalists targeted Mubarak in an assassination attempt that may have been orchestrated by al-Qaeda.[194] In the wake of September 11, Egyptian police rounded up twenty-two professionals who belonged to the banned Muslim Brotherhood, while Tunisia and other countries have sought to crack down on their own brands of politicized Islam. Algeria, for instance, has been fighting a decade-long war against Muslim fundamentalists. "Each North African country has its own bin Laden," editorialized the French-language Arab weekly *Jeune Afrique* in the wake of September 11.[195] At a 1992 meeting in Algiers, the OAU passed a resolution at its meeting calling for enhanced cooperation in fighting terrorism, and in 1999, again in Algiers, the organization adopted the Convention on the Prevention and Combating of Terrorism.[196]

Over the last decade, Sudan has been a major U.S. concern, labeled a "rogue state," denied diplomatic recognition, and placed off-limits to U.S. investors. From 1991 to 1996, bin Laden was based in the Sudan, and the al-Qaeda leader claimed his operatives were involved in the 1993 killing of American marines in Mogadishu, Somalia.[197] The United States also viewed Sudan as an operational base for al-Qaeda's August 7, 1998, simultaneous bombings of the embassies in Kenya and Tanzania that killed 224 and injured thousands, mainly Africans. In retaliation, the Clinton administration launched a cruise missile attack, destroying what it claimed was an al-Qaeda chemical weapons facility, but which subsequent investigations found was a pharmaceutical factory.[198] Yet during the 1990s, there were diplomatic crosscurrents, as Sudanese officials met secretly with the FBI and CIA in an effort to combat terrorism, even offering, according to some reports, to help apprehend bin Laden.[199] After September 11, the Khartoum government immediately announced it would cooperate in the search for Islamic terrorists and revealed publicly that U.S. intelligence agents were already operating in Sudan.[200]

In the United States, however, these steps toward engagement with Sudan's National Islamic Front government are opposed by an unlikely coalition of religious right organizations and African-American churches, human rights groups, and labor unions. They are backing Christian guerrilla groups in southern Sudan who, for nearly half a century, have been waging a civil war demanding self-determination. Complicating the political landscape, U.S. corporations, circumscribed by the embargo, have watched with frustration as Chinese and Canadian petroleum companies invested in Sudan's largely unexplored but potentially large oil reserves.[201] Once again, powerful but strange bedfellows have pushed Sudan onto the Bush administration's Africa agenda.

Libya, the North African country Washington has long considered at the top of its terrorism list, did not make it into President Bush's "axis of evil." Following the terrorist attacks, Qaddafi quickly declared that "the United States has the right to vengeance"[202] and then revealed that Libya had been providing intelligence about al-Qaeda to the United States. Yet relations between the two countries remain far from normalized. In 2003, the Bush administration extended for another year the strict trade, investment, and travel sanctions imposed on Libya in 1986 (in retaliation for the suspected Libyan bombing of a Berlin discotheque) and rejected Libya's draft statement apologizing for the 1989 terrorist bombing of Pan Am 103 over Lockerbie, Scotland. Washington's rejection of this statement, which had been accepted by both Britain and the victims' families, delayed both Libya's removal from the State Department's list of countries that sponsor terrorism and Libya's payment of compensation to the families, reported to total $2.7 billion.[203] After Iraq, one political analyst told the *New York Times*, "Libya is either No. 2 or No. 3 on the list of nations the hard-liners want to go after."[204]

The State Department's 2001 report on terrorism accurately stated that "most terrorist attacks in Africa stem from internal civil unrest and spillover from regional wars" in, for instance, the Democratic Republic of the Congo, Liberia, and Sierra Leone. However, the report noted that both al-Qaeda and the Lebanese Hizballah "have a presence in Africa and continue to exploit Africa's permissive operating environment—porous borders, conflict, lax financial systems, and the wide availability of weapons—to expand and strengthen their networks."[205] The State Department put several African insurgencies on its list of terrorist groups, including the Sudanese-backed Lord's Resistance Army in northern Uganda and the Revolutionary United Front in Sierra Leone.

As U.S. preparations for war against Iraq mounted, the Horn of Africa became an increasingly important outpost in the war on terrorism. A Navy command ship was stationed off the Horn's coast on an "open-ended mission" to "track, frustrate and eliminate" al-Qaeda terrorists.[206] By early 2003, some eight hundred U.S. special operations forces and CIA paramilitaries and fifteen hundred marines were operating from an abandoned French Foreign Legion post in tiny

Djibouti, just across the Gulf of Aden from Yemen, Osama bin Laden's ancestral homeland and the suspected hideaway of al-Qaeda operatives. This first U.S. base in Africa in the post–Cold War era is also useful for observing suspected terrorists in neighboring Somalia.[207]

Eastern Africa has also continued to be the site of al-Qaeda attacks. In November 2002, al-Qaeda claimed responsibility for a suicide car bombing at an Israeli-owned beach hotel in Mombasa (killing ten Kenyans, three Israelis, and the three bombers) and for the failed attempt to shoot down an Israeli charter jet with shoulder-launched missiles. Coming just weeks after the deadly bombing of a tourist nightclub in Bali, the Mombasa incident was part of what an al-Qaeda spokesman vowed would be a widening war against the "Christian-Jewish alliance" of the United States and Israel and its other allies.[208] Indeed, within a few weeks, the United States and other countries issued tourism travel warnings of a terrorist plot against the Muslim resort island Zanzibar.[209]

OIL AND SECURITY

One year after the September 11 attacks, the lead story in the *New York Times* proclaimed that "Africa, the neglected stepchild of American diplomacy, is rising in strategic importance to Washington policy makers, and one word sums up the reason: oil."[210] In early 2002, the newly created African Oil Policy Initiative Group (AOPIG), composed of congressional members, administration officials, industry executives, consultants, and investors, drew up a blueprint for U.S. energy and mineral resource interests in Africa. As House Subcommittee on Africa chair Ed Royce (R-CA) explained, "African oil should be treated as a priority for U.S. national security post 9-11, and I think that post 9-11 it's occurred to all of us that our traditional sources of oil are not as secure as we once thought they were."[211]

U.S. imports of crude oil from West Africa—Nigeria, Angola, Equatorial Guinea, Gabon—equal 15 percent of total imports and are set to rise to 25 percent by 2015, according to the National Intelligence Council.[212] In his 2001 National Energy Policy Report, U.S. Vice President Dick Cheney projected that the area would be "one of the fastest-growing sources of oil and gas for the American market."[213] Expansion plans include reopening the U.S. consulate in Equatorial Guinea, where off-shore reserves have been recently discovered, a new embassy in oil-rich Angola, construction of a pipeline linking southern Chad to Atlantic ports, increased military exchanges with West African countries, and a possible new U.S. naval base on Sao Tome and Principe, a tiny, two-island nation strategically located in the Atlantic oil-bearing basin of the Gulf of Guinea.

With civil war and unrest in Colombia and Venezuela, upheavals in the Middle East and war looming with Iraq, Africa was playing "an increasingly important role in our energy security," Energy Secretary Spencer Abraham told the House International Relations Committee in June 2002.[214] Shortly afterward, Secretary of State Powell was dispatched to visit Gabon, Sao Tome, and Angola, oil-rich countries that rarely, if ever, have been visited by a high-level U.S. official.[215] Powell avoided Nigeria, the most important African oil supplier to the United States, where popular resistance continues to grow against oil companies in the Niger Delta region. Quietly, however, the Bush administration has increased its military ties to Nigeria, while pressuring it to pull out of the Organization of Petroleum Exporting Countries (OPEC), the quota and price-setting cartel. As one oil industry official explained, "There is a long-term strategy from the U.S. government to weaken OPEC's hold on the market and one way to do that is to peel off certain countries."[216] By summer 2002, Bush's Africa policy was characterized as "build the military and extract the oil."[217]

While most current military training programs predate September 11, the United States has sought to strengthen relations with African police, military, and security forces in a bid to identify Islamic radicals and secure access to oil resources. At present, nearly every sub-Saharan country receives International Military Education and Training (IMET) funding.[218] U.S. Special Forces, through the African Crisis Response Initiative started in 1997, have trained eight thousand troops from Senegal, Ghana, Mali, and other countries.[219] Both South Africa and Kenya received lists of suspects from the United States and agreed to cooperate.[220]

In Kenya, a key U.S. ally from the Cold War era and central to any U.S. antiterrorist operations against Somalia, three thousand U.S. Marines participated with Kenyan troops in large-scale military exercises in February 2002. In the run-up to the December 2002 presidential elections, many Kenyans feared the expanded focus on security and counterterrorism would push democratization to the back burner. Indeed, during President Moi's final state visit to Washington in early December 2002, President Bush made no public appeal for peaceful and fair elections.[221] Despite Washington's official silence, Kenya's December elections took place without violence or corruption, and the next day Moi turned over power to opposition candidate Mwai Kibaki.[222]

While Kenya's political transition was smooth, U.S. policy makers worried that domestic conflict and social collapse in a number of African countries would provide opportunities for Islamic fundamentalists to recruit or to exploit criminal financial networks. As Africa Subcommittee Chair Ed Royce argued, "The general weakness of African governments as well as the civil strife, which

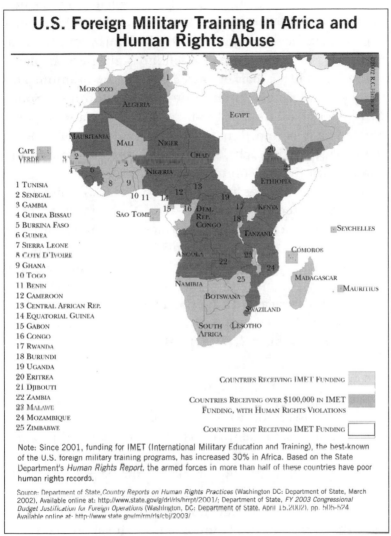

U.S. Foreign Military Training In Africa and Human Rights Abuse

1 TUNISIA
2 SENEGAL
3 GAMBIA
4 GUINEA BISSAU
5 BURKINA FASO
6 GUINEA
7 SIERRA LEONE
8 CÔTE D'IVOIRE
9 GHANA
10 TOGO
11 BENIN
12 CAMEROON
13 CENTRAL AFRICAN REP.
14 EQUATORIAL GUINEA
15 GABON
16 CONGO
17 RWANDA
18 BURUNDI
19 UGANDA
20 ERITREA
21 DJIBOUTI
22 ZAMBIA
23 MALAWI
24 MOZAMBIQUE
25 ZIMBABWE

COUNTRIES RECEIVING IMET FUNDING

COUNTRIES RECEIVING OVER $100,000 IN IMET FUNDING, WITH HUMAN RIGHTS VIOLATIONS

COUNTRIES NOT RECEIVING IMET FUNDING

Note: Since 2001, funding for IMET (International Military Education and Training), the best-known of the U.S. foreign military training programs, has increased 30% in Africa. Based on the State Department's *Human Rights Report*, the armed forces in more than half of these countries have poor human rights records.

Source: Department of State, *Country Reports on Human Rights Practices* (Washington DC: Department of State, March 2002), Available online at: http://www.state.gov/g/drl/rls/hrrpt/2001/; Department of State, *FY 2003 Congressional Budget Justification for Foreign Operations* (Washington, DC: Department of State, April 15, 2002), pp. 505-524 Available online at: http://www.state.gov/m/rm/rls/cbj/2003/

exists in several countries, makes parts of the continent hospitable grounds for terrorist operations."[223] The U.S. focus on security has brought African states with Muslim populations under close scrutiny, while military training is being expanded, new intelligence relationships are being forged, and alleged African links to global criminal networks are being probed. After September 11, reports began to surface of possible al-Qaeda connections to criminal gangs in Mozambique, diamond smugglers in Sierra Leone, and black-market purchases of raw uranium and money laundering with tanzanite gems in Tanzania. South Africa closed a number of bank accounts because of possible terrorist connections and, along with several other states, rushed through legislation on money laundering and monitoring telecommunications.

But this threat has not prompted the U.S. military to intervene directly in Africa. Post-Vietnam and post-Mogadishu (where eighteen marines were killed during a UN mission in 1993), Bush continues to oppose sending U.S. forces into Africa's several civil wars. Instead, the United States is promoting regional peacekeeping forces led by South Africa and Nigeria, a view reflected as well in the peace and security initiative of the New Partnership for Africa's Development (NEPAD).[224]

DIFFERING U.S. AND AFRICAN AGENDAS

A growing discomfort with U.S. unilateralism has increased anti-American sentiment across the continent and prompted calls for UN rather than U.S. leadership in the war on terrorism.[225] Within just two weeks of the September 2001 attacks, Egyptian President Mubarak warned that Washington's "cure should not be more bitter than the illness."[226] Terrorism is far from the most critical problem confronting the continent. Poverty, AIDS, protracted violent conflicts between countries, debt burdens, and the breakdown of states have all ranked higher on the agendas of African leaders and regional organizations. As Salih Booker, director of the U.S.-based policy organization Africa Action, wrote, "Whether measured by numbers killed or nations wounded, by economies upended or families crushed, the AIDS pandemic is a deadlier global threat than that posed by terrorist groups.... The war on AIDS is more important than the war on terrorism."[227] Yet, after September 11, the U.S. government began to look at Africa almost exclusively through the lenses of terrorism and oil.[228]

When the Bush administration took office, it signaled that Africa would remain a low priority, economically and strategically. During the Cold War, the U.S. foreign aid and alliances in Africa were largely aimed at checking Soviet and Chinese influence. In the 1990s, the Clinton administration proclaimed that free market prescriptions—trade, not aid; export-led growth; and structural adjustment policies— would define its relations with Africa. But less U.S. foreign direct investment goes to Africa than any other world region—less than one percent of the total in 2001[229]—and over half of that goes to the oil industry. And Clinton's much-touted trade access bill, the Africa Growth and Opportunity Act (AGOA), helped increase African exports (mainly textiles) to the United States for a handful of countries, including Mauritius, Lesotho, Mozambique, and Kenya.

The Bush administration continues to press African economies to privatize, open up to foreign capital, develop "good governance" practices, and uphold agreements to end conflicts in the Congo and elsewhere. At the same time, the administration has modestly increased development assistance, while favoring neoliberal protégés such as Mozambique, South Africa, and Nigeria. U.S. contributions still lag far behind Europe, and by mid-2002, the $700 million that the United States had committed for the Heavily Indebted Poor Countries Initiative had yet to be disbursed. Most of the Bush administration's $2.2 billion in total aid to Africa for 2003 was not appropriated by Congress.[230]

Meanwhile, the United States provided only a modest contribution of $200 million to the UN Global AIDS Fund, which estimates its needs at $7 to $10 billion.

By the time Americans commemorated the first anniversary of the terrorist attacks, African support and goodwill, as symbolized in the gift of cattle, had largely vanished. The Bush administration's unilateralist policies combined with its aggressive and narrow obsession with security and oil in Africa have increasingly alienated many Africans. In September 2002, Africa's most respected statesman, Nelson Mandela, charged in uncharacteristically bitter language that "the attitude of the United States is a threat to world peace." Mandela, who had supported the U.S. war in Afghanistan, lashed out at Bush officials for pursuing war in Iraq. He went a step further, charging that in the eyes of many, U.S. actions—from not paying compensation to Africans killed or injured in the two embassy bombings, to snubbing the world summits on racism and sustainable development (both held in South Africa), to showing contempt for UN Secretary General Kofi Annan—contain "that element": racism.[231] This racism, which also underlies U.S. designs on African oil, the prioritizing of counterterrorism over tackling poverty and AIDS, and the militarizing of the continent, has distorted Washington's perception of what truly matters to Africa and Africans.

LATIN AMERICA
by Coletta Youngers

FROM CHILE TO CUBA to Mexico, Latin American countries united behind Washington in the wake of the September 11 attacks. The Organization of American States (OAS) issued a declaration stating, "Individually and collectively, we will deny terrorist groups the capacity to operate in this Hemisphere. This American family stands united." Yet despite this overwhelming show of solidarity, the Bush administration has largely turned its back on its Latin American allies. Most disturbingly, it is unilaterally waging war against its own Latin American "axis of evil"—the Colombian "narcoterrorists," Cuba's Fidel Castro, and Venezuela's Hugo Chávez—with little if no effort to take into account the concerns of Latin American leaders, reach regional accords, or engage the OAS.

With the election of Luiz Inacio ("Lula") da Silva in Brazil, yet another country was added to the "axis of evil" according to conservative Representative Henry Hyde (R-IL)[232]. Upon taking office, Lula pledged to eradicate hunger in the region's largest country, a far greater threat to most Latin Americans than international terrorism, prompting Venezuelan President Hugo Chávez to proclaim an "axis of good."

U.S. policy makers have long considered the tri-border area of Argentina, Brazil, and Paraguay a hotbed of Arab radicalism, concerns fueled by bombings carried out by Hizballah in Argentina in 1992 and 1994. The most recent State Department report on terrorism still refers to the region as a "hub for Hizballah and HAMAS activities, particularly for logistical and financial purposes."[233] Arab populations in Latin America are now under close scrutiny by U.S. intelligence officials, raising serious civil rights concerns. However, alleged terrorist activity in this area of the world pales in comparison to other U.S. global priorities. In short, Latin America is near the bottom of the U.S. antiterrorist agenda.

The one exception is Colombia. Home to three groups on the U.S. State Department's list of foreign terrorist organizations and the third-largest recipient of U.S. military aid in the world, Colombia remains the centerpiece of U.S. counterterrorist efforts in the hemisphere. In the post–September 11 worldview of most Washington policy makers, the distinction between terrorists and drug traffickers operating in Colombia and other places has been obliterated. "Terrorism and drugs go together like rats and the bubonic plague," proclaims U.S. Attorney General John Ashcroft. "They thrive in the same conditions, support each other and feed off of each other."[234] The United States has consequently collapsed its antidrug and counterterrorism efforts into a single offensive.

U.S. POLICY TOWARD THE REGION

Across Latin America, a general malaise has set in due to the never-ending and escalating economic crisis, deep-rooted corruption, and the inability of democracy to truly take root. Years of following Washington's prescribed free-market economic policies have not only failed to pay off, the region has moved backward—poverty has increased, privatizations have led to rampant corruption and often skyrocketing prices for basic services, and inequality is worse than ever. The combination of economic and political instability can be deadly for weak governments, as was so brutally illustrated in the protests in Argentina in December 2001 that brought down the de la Rúa government. Yet the Bush administration's response to the Argentina crisis is symbolic of its present approach to the region. Like an angry father, former Treasury Secretary Paul O'Neill scolded Argentina and suggested that it get its own house in order, and the rest of the Bush administration largely adopted a similar tone.[235]

This may not be what President Bush intended upon assuming office, when he promised to develop a special relationship with Latin America and with Mexico in particular. Encouraged by Mexican President Vicente Fox and fueled by the desire to capture more of the Hispanic vote at home, the Bush administration began moving in the direction of a radical reform of U.S. immigration policy, which could have significantly reshaped not only U.S.-Mexican relations, but also, more broadly, U.S.-Latin American relations. All of this, however, was derailed by September 11.

U.S. policy toward the region in the wake of September 11 has largely returned to the "rollback" framework adopted by the Reagan administration at the height of the Cold War. Latin America is viewed as a region where "terrorist" threats are to be eliminated, particularly in the tumultuous Andean countries and Communist Cuba. As such, the region is viewed not as an opportunity for constructive international engagement but as a threat.[236] This strategy was unleashed full force in the wake of September 11. Speaking of Colombia, Representative Henry Hyde (R-IL), chairman of the House International Relations Committee, went so far as to warn that "three hours by plane from Miami, we face a potential breeding ground for international terror equaled perhaps only by Afghanistan. The threat to American national interest is both imminent and clear."[237] Nonetheless, since September 11, very little engagement by high-level U.S. officials—with the occasional exception of Colombia—has occurred.

The Bush administration's approach departs somewhat from that of its predecessor. While the Clinton administration also adopted a get-tough approach to "narco-terrorists" and dramatically increased U.S. military involvement in Colombia, it at least rhetorically limited the mission to counter-narcotics and paid lip service to the Colombian peace process. More broadly, it placed greater emphasis on multilateral mechanisms and regional consensus-building in approaching conflict situations and issues such as the environment that are not on the Bush administration's radar screen.

Greater continuity is evident in the pursuit of U.S. economic interests. Both the Clinton and Bush administrations have pursued free trade agreements to ensure U.S. economic dominance of the hemisphere and to promote U.S. business interests. The Bush administration also views the region as a source of oil and oil profits. In both Mexico and Venezuela, it has encouraged changes in legal and constitutional restrictions on foreign investment in domestic oil production and has sought to increase imports to the United States. Mexico has responded cautiously to such overtures, while Venezuelan President Hugo Chávez repeatedly rebuffed them.[238]

THE VENEZUELA DEBACLE

Indeed, the Bush administration's first major foreign policy debacle in the region took place in Venezuela as a result of an apparent military-led coup against President Chávez. Several days of business and labor protests in that country culminated in a massive march on April 11, 2002, in which unidentified gunmen killed at least eighteen people. Chávez's foes moved against him later that night, taking Chávez prisoner and announcing his resignation from office. Business leader Pedro Carmona was asked to head the unconstitutional, military-installed government. Carmona's rise to power, however, was short-lived. Within two days, Chávez, who claimed never to have resigned, was back in the presidential palace.

In stark contrast to its attitude toward most Latin American governments, the Bush administration immediately accepted the illegitimate Carmona government, issuing an unusually undiplomatic statement on April 12 that blamed Chávez for his own fall. U.S. involvement in the coup attempt itself is not at all clear; however, it does appear that the administration had decided that Chávez had to go.

As the fourth-largest supplier of U.S. crude oil to the United States, Venezuela has been an obvious target for U.S. hegemonic designs, particularly in light of Chávez's preferred policy of cutting production to keep prices high. Moreover, Chávez had angered many in Washington with his overtures to "rogue" rulers in Iraq, Libya, and particularly Cuba.

Months prior to the coup, a steady stream of Venezuelan opposition leaders made their way to Washington, many with the support of the National Endowment for Democracy, the Center for Strategic and International Studies, and right-wing think tanks. They met with a range of U.S. officials who, while maintaining opposition to an outright coup, likely made it clear that they would very much like "Chávez to go away," ideally via a constitutional maneuver.[239] A strong message of support for some sort of action was sent.

The Bush administration's quick embrace of the short-lived Carmona government was criticized across the region, providing "Latin Americans cause to wonder," according to analyst David Corn, "if the United States is continuing its tradition of underhandedly meddling in the affairs of its neighbors to the south."[240] It also sent a dangerous message about the weak U.S. commitment to democratic principles. The U.S. stance toward Chávez, as well as interventions in electoral campaigns in Nicaragua, Bolivia, and Brazil in favor of or in opposition to particular candidates, sends the very clear message that Washington supports electoral democracy—as long as its candidate wins.

CASTRO'S CUBA

The impact on the Bush administration of Chávez's relations with Cuba's Fidel Castro cannot be underestimated. The appointment of Otto Reich as President Bush's first assistant secretary of state for Latin America was widely interpreted as a payback to the conservative, Miami-based Cuban-American community for its support of Bush in the Florida recount, as well as "pay-forward for their continued support in the 2002 gubernatorial and congressional elections."[241] A Cuban-American and former lobbyist for Bacardi, Reich has strong ties to that community. Despite growing support on Capitol Hill for a reform of U.S. policy toward Cuba, the Bush administration has remained firm in its commitment to the U.S. economic embargo and to continued isolation of the Cuban government, with no significant policy change likely in the foreseeable future.

In an explosive speech before the Heritage Foundation on May 6, 2002, John Bolton, undersecretary for arms control and international security, went even further, bluntly stating: "The United States believes that Cuba has at least a limited offensive biological warfare research and development effort. Cuba has provided dual-use biotechnology to other rogue states." He also noted that Castro had recently visited Iran, Syria, and Libya, all states designated by Washington as sponsors of terrorism. Administration officials frequently repeat a statement allegedly made by Castro on his visit to Iran that operating together, Iran and Cuba could "bring America to its knees."[242] Bolton offered no evidence to support his assertions of biological warfare, which were quickly deflated by former president Jimmy Carter's historic May 2002 trip to Cuba. Carter said that he was told by U.S. officials that "there was no evidence linking Cuba to the export of biological weaponry,"[243] and while in Cuba, he was given complete access to the country's biomedical facilities.

THE COLOMBIAN QUAGMIRE

The U.S. government is seeking to expand its hegemonic reach across the Andean region, driven in part by the politi-

The Impact of the U.S. Embargo on Cuba's Health and Nutrition

Drugs and Medical Equipment: The Cuban Democracy Act (1992), by forbidding foreign subsidiaries of U.S. companies from selling to Cuba, posed new and almost insurmountable obstacles to the sale of medicines and medical supplies.

Food Security: U.S. sanctions reduce Cuba's import capacity for basic foodstuffs. Shipping regulations and the ban on direct and subsidiary trade in food close Cuba off from an otherwise natural market.

Water Quality: The embargo contributes to serious cutbacks in supplies of safe drinking water and was a factor in the increase in morbidity rates in the 1990s.

HIV Infection and AIDS: The embargo limits access to life-prolonging drugs for Cuban HIV/AIDS patients, and otherwise impairs prevention, diagnosis, treatment, and research in this field.

Women's Health: The U.S. embargo directly contributes to lapses in prevention, diagnosis, therapeutic and surgical treatments of breast cancer; diminished alternatives for contraception; gaps in availability of in-vitro genetic testing resources; reduced access to medications associated with pregnancy, labor and delivery; and deficient nutrition during pregnancy.

Children's Health: Cuba's economic crisis, exacerbated by embargo restrictions, exacts a toll on children's health, particularly in neonatology, immunizations, pediatric hospital care, access to medicines, and treatment of acute illnesses.

Hospital Care: The economic crisis and the U.S. embargo have seriously eroded surgery, radiology, clinical services, and access to medication, hospital nutrition, and hygiene.

Oncology: The U.S. embargo bars Cubans' access to state-of-the-art cancer treatment under U.S. patent, subjects all diagnosis and treatment-related imports to delays due to the shipping ban, and hinders domestic research, development, and production due to the ban on biotech-related exports.

Cardiology: The U.S. embargo constitutes a direct threat to patient care, by denying Cuban heart patients access to lifesaving medications and equipment only available in the United States.

Nephrology: The embargo limits the chance of survival of Cuban patients with chronic renal failure, increases their suffering, and adds significant expense to already costly care.

Professional Advancement and Scientific Information: The embargo remains a formidable barrier to the free flow of ideas and scientific information between Cuban medical researchers and their colleagues in the United States.

Humanitarian Donations: Donations do not compensate to any major degree for the hardships inflicted by the embargo on the health of the Cuban people. There are restrictions placed on charitable donations from the United States, similar to those placed on commercial trade. Contributions rarely match needs in terms of specific drugs, equipment, or replacement parts.

Source: American Association of World Health, "The Impact of the U.S. Embargo on Health and Nutrition in Cuba," 1997.

cal and economic instability of all of the Andean countries and the potential for "spillover" of the Colombian conflict into bordering countries. Otto Reich, later named special envoy to the Americas, likes to point out that if the so-called narco-guerrillas were to "ever gain control over larger parts of Colombian territories, I think there is no doubt that they will take their business, which is narcotics and terrorism, to other countries."[244] In short, the Revolutionary Armed Forces of Colombia (FARC) have become the al-Qaeda of Latin America.

As noted, three of the thirty-five groups listed by the State Department as of October 2002 as foreign terrorist organizations are in Colombia: the FARC, the National Liberation Army (ELN), and the right-wing paramilitary coalition, the United Self-Defense Groups of Colombia (AUC).[245] In 2001, more kidnappings took place in Colombia than any other country in the world. Since 1980, the FARC has killed at least ten American citizens and three more remain unaccounted for.[246] Former U.S. ambassador to Colombia Curtis Kamman sums up: "The terrorists who operate in Colombia have not explicitly declared the United States to be their target. But their political and economic objectives are incompatible with our values, and they could ultimately represent a force for evil no less troublesome than Al Qaeda or irresponsible forces possessing weapons of mass destruction."[247]

U.S. interest in Colombia began long before September 11. In the name of the war on drugs, the U.S. government provided Colombia with $1.7 billion as part of "Plan Colombia." However, in the wake of September 11 and congressional acquiescence to combat terrorism abroad in virtually any form, the administration moved quickly to expand the mission in Colombia to provide direct counterinsurgency assistance and intelligence. It requested for FY 2003 almost half a billion

A Sharp Increase

The Bush Administration's "Andean Regional Initiative" aid request for 2003 brings a jump in military and police aid for Colombia's neighbors.

Panama:
2000-2001 average: $3.5 million
2003 request: $8.6 million
Change: +146%

Venezuela:
2000-2001 average: $4.9 million
2003 request: $8.6 million
Change: +76%

Colombia:
2000-2001 average: $569.9 million
2003 request: $754.7 million
Change: +32%

Ecuador:
2000-2001 average: $18.9 million
2003 request: $33.1 million
Change: +75%

Brazil:
2000-2001 average: $3.8 million
2003 request: $11.9 million
Change: +213%

Peru:
2000-2001 average: $25.8 million
2003 request: $71.2 million
Change: +176%

Bolivia:
2000-2001 average: $48.2 million
2003 request: $52.5 million
Change: +9%

2003 request figures are taken from State Department Foreign Operations requests, plus estimates of counternarcotics drawdowns and Defense Department assistance.

dollars in aid to Colombia, 70 percent of which is for the nation's military and police forces.[218]

A central component of the expanded mission would protect U.S. oil interests in Colombia. The administration intends to provide $98 million for the army to protect the Caño Limon-Coveñas pipeline, operated by the California-based Occidental Petroleum and carrying oil for export to the United States. While details of the plan are still sketchy, military officials at the embassy confirm that U.S. advisers plan to train three well-equipped hundred-man army units "to act as rapid deployment forces" when guerrilla forces attack the pipeline.[249] The pipeline, to be protected by what the Bush administration has dubbed the "Critical Infrastructure Brigade," provides Occidental Petroleum with profits from 35 million barrels of oil a year, for which it pays about fifty cents per barrel in security costs. The cost to the U.S. taxpayer amounts to three dollars a barrel—in short, a rather hefty taxpayer subsidy for Occidental Petroleum.[250]

A POLITICAL ALTERNATIVE?

The shift in policy in Washington coincides conveniently with changing political winds in Colombia. As the faltering peace process embarked upon by former president Pastrana finally collapsed and FARC violence escalated, Colombians voted overwhelmingly for hard-line candidate Alvaro Uribe, who promised to wage all-out war against what he calls terrorism by armed groups. Quietly backed by right-wing paramilitary groups, Uribe is not likely to take action against either their attacks on civilian populations perceived to be supporting the guerrillas or the elements of the military that support them. Upon taking office in August 2002, he immediately moved to roll back civil liberties and human rights protections in the name of his domestic war on terrorism.
Yet in embarking upon a purely military strategy, Uribe risks repeating the failed strategies of the past. Nearly four decades of civil conflict have shown that the war will not be won on the battlefield. Each day that a political settlement is postponed, dozens of Colombians are killed, disappeared, or internally displaced. While there is no quick fix to the conflict, the two fundamental pillars of any long-term solution are a political accord and socioeconomic development programs that address the underlying causes of violence.

For its part, Washington should take a cold, hard look at the long-term implications of its decision to slide down the slippery slope of direct involvement in Colombia's brutal civil war. As aptly noted by Republican Congressman Ron Paul (R-TX), "I can't conceive of us sending tens of thousands of soldiers down there. But we are down there because we are determined to get involved in their civil war, and it could become a little Vietnam."[251]

Washington needs to adopt a dramatically different approach to Latin America, one that turns around the asymmetrical balance of power between the two and incorporates Latin American viewpoints into U.S. foreign policy. Were they to do so, U.S. policy makers would quickly recognize that the greatest threat to hemispheric peace and security is persistent poverty and inequality. Poverty elimination and the provision of economic assistance—in a way that allows countries to determine their own economic and development policies—should be the centerpiece of U.S. policy toward Latin America and the Caribbean. Perhaps most important, the challenge for U.S. policy makers is to move beyond containing and rolling back perceived threats and work instead toward the construction of a common vision of what could be: a hemisphere united around shared prosperity, respect for basic human rights, and citizen participation in democratic government.

ASIA

by John Gershman

ASIA IS ARGUABLY the region that has been most dramatically affected by the shift in U.S. policy since the attacks of September 11. U.S. bases have cropped up in Central Asia for the first time in history. Five Japanese vessels participated in the multinational naval contingent that was part of Operation Enduring Freedom in Afghanistan, marking the first wartime dispatch of naval vessels for operations abroad since the end of World War II.[252] The Bush administration has improved relations with both Pakistan and India at the same time, a feat never accomplished during the Cold War. The administration has expanded military cooperation with Taiwan that is unprecedented since the normalization of relations with the People's Republic of China. And the United States has improved military relations with the Philippines to the closest they've been since the end of the Cold War, and begun to reengage in a significant fashion with the Indonesian military for the first time since ties were cut in 1999.

The Bush administration came into office committed to change U.S. policy toward Asia. It aimed at reversing the Clinton-era policies of engagement with North Korea and China, and strengthening military alliances perceived as having been slighted under Clinton, particularly with Japan, but also with Australia, South Korea, the Philippines, and Thailand. Military and security issues were slated to displace economics as the priority concerns of U.S. policy toward the region.

After the September 11 attacks and the launch of the Bush administration's "war on terrorism," U.S. policy toward the region followed three uneven phases. The first phase covered the period following the attacks through the State of the Union address in January 2002 and largely involved assembling a coalition that would support (or at least not oppose) the U.S.-led war in Afghanistan. The second phase was marked by two events: the identification of the "axis of evil" in the State of the Union address and the launch of the so-called "second front" in the war on terrorism in Southeast Asia. In the third and most recent phase, signs of open dissent are appearing within the administration and between the administration and its hard-line supporters concerning the administration's relationship with China. In addition, developments in the region as a whole are complicating U.S. efforts to implement its militarized foreign policies and maintain supremacy in Asia.

MILITARY PARTNERSHIP WITH JAPAN

Since the end of the Cold War, U.S.-Japan relations as a whole have been characterized by the absence of a strategic framework—a gap that the Bush administration has begun to fill. In the first phase of the "war on terrorism," the United States has put pressure on Japan to change the way it thinks of war and peace.

The closest thing to a blueprint for the Bush administration's approach to Japan can be found in the so-called Armitage Report, the product of a study group led by former Clinton administration official Joseph Nye and current Deputy Secretary of State Richard Armitage.[253] The Report places security at the center of the U.S.-Japan relationship and conceives of the U.S.-Japan security alliance as the primary anchor for U.S. force projection in the Pacific and Indian Oceans. Despite the thirty-five thousand ground troops in South Korea, no naval forces are based there. Japan hosts the only home port for a carrier battle group outside the United States, a complete amphibious attack group, and a full marine expeditionary force.

The Bush administration wants a more substantial military partnership that would begin to parallel relations with its European allies, but there is no evidence that most Japanese want such a relationship. In a stark contrast to the Bush administration, Japan's foreign policy places a greater emphasis on multilateralism. Japan has signed the landmine treaty, the Comprehensive Test Ban Treaty, and other multi-lateral arms control efforts and remains upset by the Bush administration's rejection of the Kyoto Protocol. At a minimum, however, the administration will push Japan further toward collective defense, steps foreshadowed in the late 1990s by Japan's approval of the revised U.S.-Japan security guidelines and its agreement to cooperate in pursuing theater missile defense.[254] Anything involving a more formal military role for Japan in the region remains controversial both within Japan and among many of its Asian neighbors, including those friendly to Washington, such as South Korea. Most countries in the region see a more militarily assertive Japan, given its past military adventures, as destabilizing and dangerous.

THE "AXIS OF EVIL" AND BEYOND

The second phase of the "war on terrorism" in Asia has centered on confronting North Korea and expanding the conflict to Southeast Asia. With North Korea, the Bush administration has most clearly departed from the policies of its predecessor. One of the Clinton administration's few unqualified foreign policy successes was the negotiation of the Agreed Framework in 1994, under which North Korea agreed to freeze its nuclear program in exchange for heavy fuel oil shipments and the construction of two nuclear reactors. When the United States followed the lead of South Korean President Kim Dae Jung's "sunshine policy" of engagement with the North, tensions fell to their lowest levels since the end of the Korean War.

Colin Powell advocated continuing the Clinton-era policies of engagement, but he was overruled by hard-liners soon after Bush entered office and a review of policy toward North Korea was launched.[255] Bush embarrassed

President Kim by criticizing his sunshine policy when he visited Washington in March 2001. The events of September 11 might have sparked a U.S.–North Korean rapprochement. After condemning the attacks, North Korea promptly announced that it would sign the remaining international antiterrorism conventions that it hadn't already ratified. But the United States kept North Korea on its terrorism list and maintained the accompanying economic sanctions. This more confrontational stance culminated with North Korea's inclusion in the axis of evil in the 2002 State of the Union address, even though the U.S. State Department claims North Korea hasn't engaged in terrorism since the 1980s.

In late August, the two Koreas reached an agreement on three major joint economic projects, including reconnecting severed cross-border railways, constructing an industrial complex, and instituting antiflood measures. Following Koizumi's historic trip in mid-September, Japan and North Korea began negotiations over normalizing relations. Assistant Secretary of State for East Asia James Kelly traveled to North Korea in early October and at that meeting confronted North Korean officials with evidence that it has engaged in a secret nuclear weapons program since 1997 in violation of the Agreed Framework, a charge that North Korean officials acknowledged to be true.

The crisis continued through early 2003, as North Korea restarted a small reactor at Yongbyon that could produce enough plutonium for five or six atomic weapons within a year, expelled inspectors from the International Atomic Energy Agency, and withdrew from the Nuclear Non Proliferation Treaty. Hawks within and outside the administration have used the crisis as an opportunity to attack engagement more broadly, calling for sanctions on North Korea and encouraging Japan and perhaps even South

Korea to develop their own nuclear deterrents. But key governments in the region—China, Japan, and South Korea—have called for negotiations and opposed sanctions and other efforts to isolate North Korea. The Bush administration's policy toward North Korea has only deepened South Korean opposition to the thirty-seven thousand U.S. soldiers stationed there. The December 2002 election of a new South Korean president—Roh Moo-hyun, an ardent advocate of dialogue with the North—highlights how out of step Bush administration policies are with the people most likely to be affected by any conflict with North Korea.

North Korea's acknowledgment of the weapons program, like its acknowledgment that it had abducted Japanese citizens in the 1970s and 1980s, seems aimed at a broader dialogue with the Bush administration. As of early 2003, the Bush administration continues to be divided as to how to respond to the recent developments. (The State Department itself is divided, as Undersecretary for Arms Control and International Security John Bolton continues to wave the flag of the "axis of evil" in contrast to the more positive views articulated by Powell, Deputy Secretary of State Armitage, and Assistant Secretary Kelly.)[256] The eagerness of hard-liners like Bolton to destroy the strategy of engagement represented by the Agreed Framework could provoke a replay of the 1994 nuclear crisis that brought the peninsula to the edge of war. Although the future of the Agreed Framework may be in doubt, key countries in the region continue to favor the engagement approach.

In Southeast Asia, meanwhile, the United States has focused its war on terrorism in the Philippines and Indonesia. In Indonesia, military cooperation is back on the table despite congressional opposition on the grounds of Indonesian military complicity in massive human rights abuses. Pressure from proponents of increased aid grew after the October 2002 terrorist bombings in Bali, even though it was the police, not the military, that captured some of the perpetrators. Increased military aid to Indonesia is typically justified on the basis that it will promote democracy, but the International Crisis Group (among many others) has argued that bilateral military ties have not succeeded in "producing an Indonesian military that meets the standards of a modern, professional force under civilian control."[257]

In the Philippines, the United States deployed over a thousand troops in a partially successful hostage rescue–cum–counterterrorist operation in southern Philippines. Against the backdrop of these counterterrorism operations, the United States has been transforming the Philippines into a staging area for "power projection" in the region (primarily against China/Taiwan), but also to boost projection into Central Asia and the Middle East. In August 2002 the Bush administration added the Communist Party of the Philippines and its armed wing, the New People's Army, to the State Department's list of foreign terrorist organizations. The most immediate effect was to get the Dutch government to freeze the assets of the Party leadership, which remains there in self-imposed exile. The longer-term agenda is likely to include an expansion of training and exercises to be directed at countering the nearly thirty-five–year-old insurgency. Indeed, the military training exercises scheduled to begin in October 2002 are no longer aimed at Abu Sayyaf, the Muslim separatist group linked to al-Qaeda, but will take place elsewhere in the archipelago.

The Bush administration foray into Southeast Asia has been troubling for several reasons. First, the terrorist threat was never as large as the rhetoric suggested. While there is a small network of individuals and organizations involved in terrorist activities, they have no mass following. They represent a law enforcement, not a military, challenge.[258] Second, U.S. military aid is strengthening unaccountable and repressive militaries. It also risks undermining fragile democratic institutions and legitimating broader crackdowns on political dissent by regional leaders.

CONFRONTING CHINA

In the first draft of the 1992 Defense Policy Guidance drafted by prominent U.S. hawks, it was unclear where a new rival to U.S. supremacy would most likely emerge. Europe and Japan as well as China were among the candidates. By the time the Bush administration came into office, however, the proponents of this doctrine of supremacy saw only one possible peer competitor emerging in the foreseeable future: China.[259]

But the Bush administration was divided on its approach to China from the moment it took office. Hard-line neoconservatives such as Secretary of Defense Donald Rumsfeld, his deputy Paul Wolfowitz, and Undersecretary of Defense Dov Zakheim represented a fairly unified Pentagon with John Bolton as a key outpost in the State Department. They have been backed by an even more rabid informal network of China-bashers known as the "Blue Team" who are based in congressional staff, right-wing think tanks, and media outlets. In the more moderate realpolitik camp have been Secretary of State Colin Powell, Director of the State Department's Policy Planning Staff Richard Haass, Deputy Secretary of State Richard Armitage, and Assistant Secretary of State James Kelly. National Security Adviser Condoleeza Rice, while largely siding with the hawks, has played a balancing role on policy toward China.

Early in the administration, the hawks appeared ascendant, their rhetoric considerably sharper than that of the Clinton administration. Bush denounced Clinton's efforts to forge a "strategic partnership" with China, referring instead to China as a "strategic competitor."[260] The Clintonesque pattern of engagement did prevail at key points, however, such as the negotiated resolution of the April 2001 imbroglio involving the PC-3 spy plane collision. And through September 11 that approach appears to have been maintained. Most notably, President Bush met with Chinese President Jiang Zemin twice in four months (October 2001 and February 2002) and again in October 2002. The number and frequency of these meetings are unprecedented in U.S.-China relations.

The hawks have not given up. In the wake of the spy plane incident, the Pentagon halted military ties, which as of September 2002 had yet to return to pre–April 2001 levels. Rumsfeld remains the only major cabinet member not to have met with his Chinese counterpart. Having apparently lost the intra-administration battle over how to conduct direct relations with China, the Pentagon has focused on upgrading relations with Taiwan and other allies in the region. (While it contains proponents of Taiwan independence, the Bush administration does not formally advocate this position.) In the midst of the spy plane negotiations in April 2001, the Bush administration approved the most generous arms package for Taiwan in a decade, including destroyers, antisubmarine planes, and diesel submarines. While Bush administration rhetoric with respect to Taiwan became less strident after September 11, the Pentagon quietly continued to forge closer links between the U.S. and Taiwanese military establishments, culminating in a meeting between Wolfowitz and Taiwan's minister of defense and a higher profile for U.S. military observers at Taiwan's military exercises.

The Blue Team, relatively quiet since September 11, renewed their salvos in mid-2002.[261] These China-bashers saw an opportunity in the distractions of the Chinese leadership's succession process to strengthen U.S.-Taiwan ties and heighten the anti-China tone of the renewed military ties in the region. They want a more explicit return to the framework of China as a strategic competitor, a view expressed in the first report of the U.S.-China Security Review Commission, which was staffed by a number of Blue Team members.[262] The Blue Team supports pending congressional legislation that demands greater planning and operational integration of the U.S. and Taiwanese militaries that would, if passed, contravene nearly twenty-five years of U.S. policy toward China and ignite a major crisis in U.S.-China relations.

The Asian Arms Race: U.S. Arms Sales to Taiwan

President George W. Bush decided on April 23rd 2001 to offer Taiwan the largest U.S. arms package in the last decade. The $4 billion arms package exceeds the minimum necessary to insure a balance of power in the Taiwan Strait. And as a result, China might be encouraged to spend more on new weapons, stimulating a more intense arms race in East Asia—to the detriment of everyone in the region.

The arms package includes:

- 8 diesel-electric submarines
- 12 P-3C Orion anti-submarine warfare aircraft
- 54 Mark-48 ASW torpedoes
- 44 Harpoon submarine-launched anti-ship cruse missiles
- 144 M109A6 Paladin self-propelled howitzers
- 54 AAV7A1 amphibious assault vehicles
- AN/ALE-50 electronic countermeasure systems for F-16s
- 12 MH-53 mine-sweeping helicopters
- 4 Kidd-class destroyers
- 30 AH-64D Apache Longbow attack helicopters

Source: Shirley A. Kan, *Taiwan: Major Arms Sales Since 1990* (Washington, DC: Congressional Research Service, updated September 10, 2002); James H. Nolt, "Assessing New U.S. Arms Sales to Taiwan," *Foreign Policy In Focus Commentary,* April 2001.

CHALLENGES FROM THE REGION

The aftermath of September 11 enabled the United States to expand its military presence throughout the Asia-Pacific region through military operations, exercises, aid, and training programs that have consolidated the U.S. hegemonic military presence and deepened military cooperation in the region. The net effect of these expanded ties has been to expand the capacity for U.S. force projection and to undermine democracy by strengthening unaccountable and repressive militaries in countries such as Indonesia and the Philippines. These developments were not "caused" by September 11—that is, these were not new policy initiatives—but the way the Bush administration responded to September 11 created a window of opportunity for already existing proposals to succeed.

If the events of September 11 had not happened, it is by no means clear that political support would have existed for expanded ties with the authoritarian regime in Pakistan or the chronically repressive militaries in the Philippines and Indonesia, either in the United States or in those countries. Nor would economic resources—military and foreign aid for the Philippines and Indonesia as well as debt relief for Pakistan—have been as forthcoming. These new relationships are driven by the Pentagon. The State Department remains a junior partner and has no significant resources to offer for fighting poverty or strengthening civilian democratic institutions. At the same time, key policies toward Asia have continued regardless of September 11. The September 11 attacks did nothing to weaken the Bush administration's support for national and theater missile defense systems, or its willingness to sell arms to and develop closer military ties with Taiwan.

In this third phase of the "war on terrorism," the internal conflict between the hard-liners and the advocates of engagement, unsustainable in the long term, will continue until one side or the other is defeated (with most of the betting on Colin Powell to resign first).[263] The Pentagon has the edge, since the recent boost in military spending gives it resources that other agencies lack. The most likely pressure for change in the foreseeable future will come not from within the Bush administration but from the region. A number of key events will take place in late 2002 and 2003—China's leadership succession, presidential elections in South Korea, and the decision to continue or abrogate the Agreed Framework. If Japan and South Korea continue to advocate negotiations to deal with North Korea, and continuing economic crisis makes a major expansion of Japan's military role more difficult, U.S. hard-liners will find it more difficult to promote confrontation with North Korea. Growing popular opposition throughout the region, both to the U.S. military presence and the Bush administration's increasingly aggressive and unilateralist strategic posture, has raised the costs for governments in the region to support the hard-liners' initiatives. The missing element is popular mobilization at home to seize the opportunity presented by the divide within the administration. Popular mobilization forced Congress to cut ties with the Indonesian military in 1999, and popular mobilization can challenge, transform, or at the very least mitigate the worst elements of Bush administration policy in the region.

CHAPTER FIVE

The Response

by John Feffer

THE HEADLINE IN the French newspaper *Le Monde* on September 12, 2001—"We Are All Americans"—summed up the world's reaction to the attacks on America. Expressions of great sympathy came from virtually everyone, including those generally unsympathetic to the United States such as the left-leaning *Le Monde*. Even North Korea and Iran, countries that the Bush administration would later include in the "axis of evil," condemned the attacks.

September 11 and the days following therefore represent a sharp discontinuity in the international response to the Bush administration. In its first eight months in office, the Bush policy of unilateralism—applied to arms control agreements, environmental pacts, and international institutions—received sharp censure from critics abroad and at home. In the months following the attack, as these unilateral tendencies metastasized and the U.S.-led "war on terrorism" threatened to spread to every corner of the globe, the criticisms returned in force. Only on September 11 and in the immediate aftermath did the United States, in its mourning, appear beyond criticism.

Examined more carefully, however, this apparent moratorium on criticism becomes somewhat more complicated. Take, for instance, the headline of Jean-Marie Colombani's article in *Le Monde*, which cropped up in politicians' speeches, appeared in compilations of international opinion, and was sprinkled widely around the Web. The text of the article, however, was generally ignored, perhaps because its empathetic tone was not unalloyed. "America, in the solitude of its power, in its status as the sole superpower, now in the absence of a Soviet counter-model, has ceased to draw other nations to itself; or more precisely, in certain parts of the globe, it seems to draw nothing but hate," wrote Colombani.[264] Reactions that generated firestorms of protest in the United States, whether Susan Sontag's reflections in *The New Yorker* or Bill Maher's politically incorrect comments, were a great deal more common overseas.[265]

September 11 has been billed as a discontinuity in a more significant way. "This day has changed the world," German President Johannes Rau said in the wake of the tragedy, a sentiment echoed by newspapers and politicians the world over.[266] In some respects this is clearly true. The United States, like Europe, now feels vulnerable to large-scale terrorist attacks, New York has experienced death and destruction like Nablus or Tel Aviv, and U.S. security organs seem as incapable of anticipating or preventing such devastating attacks as any of their less well-funded counterparts around the world. In another important sea change, Germany and Japan, in contributing troops to the war in Afghanistan, have now shrugged off post–World War II constraints on their national armies to become "normal" nations.

But a year and a half later, the continuities connecting the periods before and after September 11 are perhaps more salient. European nations are still uncomfortable with U.S. militarism; Russia and China are engaged in a subtle geopolitical ménage à trois with the United States to preserve their own regional power; countries in the developing world wonder if they will be the next in line for preemptive U.S. strikes after the Taliban and Saddam Hussein; the United Nations is still trying to restrain the United States with the fraying threads of multilateralism. The United States has been here before. International criticisms of the U.S. execution of its war on terrorism not surprisingly echo past outcries, whether from Europe over U.S. strikes against Libya in 1986 or from Arab countries over U.S. missile attacks against Sudan and Afghanistan in 1998. Unilateralism runs deep in American foreign policy, and it is through the mirror of foreign opinion that Americans can perhaps best glimpse this uncomfortable truth.

EUROPEAN HESITATIONS

Initially September 11 seemed to revivify transatlantic relations. European leaders rushed to support the Bush administration, and thirty hours after the attack NATO invoked Article 5, authorizing its troops to respond to an attack on one of its members. NATO planes helped protect U.S. airspace after September 11. Europe welcomed the diplomatic attempts of Colin Powell to build a united front for the attack on al-Qaeda and the Taliban. Britain sent their special forces, Germany contributed three thousand troops, and French planes flew the second-largest number of sorties over Afghanistan.[267] European governments froze $35 million in assets of suspected terrorists and cooperated in the hunt for al-Qaeda cells and operatives.[268]

This show of support, however, concealed a Euro-American breach that shared tragedy could not mend. To expedite its response to September 11, the United States sidestepped the challenges of coalition work—the dreaded "war by committee" conducted either through NATO or the European Union—and followed a pattern of multiple bilateralism by which U.S. officials worked directly with national capitals.[269] For the war on Iraq, the Bush administration managed to persuade only Britain and Spain. If this trend toward multiple bilateralism continues, the United States may well transform transatlantic relations along transpacific lines. In Asia, bilateral ties between the United States and Japan, South Korea, the Philippines, Australia, and Thailand substitute for a multilateral security framework.

Europe shows signs of resisting this Pacificization of the Euro-American relationship. European leaders are well aware of the U.S. strategy, leaked to the press in 1992, of discouraging "the advanced industrial nations from challenging our leadership or...even aspiring to a larger regional or global role."[270] The European Union boasts a new currency, is about to absorb ten new members and may grow to more than thirty by the end of the decade, and generally pursues a different approach than the United States to a range of problems from global poverty to global warming. European countries bristle at being treated as irrelevant, weak-kneed, or insufficiently mature. As one EU official put it, "It is humiliating and demeaning if we feel we have to go and get our homework marked by Dick Cheney and Condi Rice."[271] These frustrations, coming to a head in the late 1990s, pushed the Europeans to explore an independent military capability, the European Security and Defense Policy (ESDP), backed up by a sixty-thousand-strong rapid reaction force. The creation of this force by the target date of 2003 is unlikely because of internal politics,[272] but few doubt that Europe will eventually develop what Dutch Prime Minister Wim Kok and others have championed, namely a "counterweight to the United States."[273]

European frustrations are intensified by feelings of impotence. "America is waking up to the huge preponderance of its military power," editorialized *The Economist*. "Europe, realising this, is worried both about the wise application of that power, and its own relative weakness."[274] The Bush administration's 2002 military budget increase of $48 billion is twice the size of the German military budget. In the early 1990s, it was not uncommon for analysts to predict the formation of three roughly equal blocs of power defined more by economic than military might—the European Union, the North American Free Trade Area, and the yen bloc.[275] While economic power is distributed more evenly among industrialized countries, military might remains the domain of the United States, and Europeans are being relegated to peacekeeping and humanitarian tasks.[276] Disagreements over trade, which have proven so acrimonious in the past, will only intensify in such an atmosphere of resentment.

European countries became even more uncomfortable with U.S. policy as a localized strike against the Taliban and al-Qaeda quickly became a global war. The January 2002 "axis of evil" speech marked a turning point in European reactions. Tony Blair and conservative prime ministers in Italy and Spain applauded Bush's words. Everyone else was appalled. Viewed from Brussels or Bonn, there is no axis of evil, just three very difficult diplomatic challenges. With the exception of Ireland and France, every member of the EU has extended diplomatic recognition to North Korea, and the EU has strongly backed the engagement policy of South Korean president Kim Dae Jung. European leaders have reached out to moderates in Iran, setting up a comprehensive dialogue on nonproliferation, human rights, and trade (the EU is Iran's major trading partner).[277] And European countries, with the exception of Britain and Spain, went to great lengths to avoid a war with Iraq.

Europe and the United States also look at terrorism very differently. Europeans put more stress on addressing the root causes of terrorism, which is not surprising, since countries such as Britain and Spain have been forced to approach their own "terrorists" with more than mere firepower. European leaders have stressed the importance of addressing global poverty in the wake of September 11, but such calls, even from Bush ally Tony Blair, have "found little resonance in Washington, DC."[278] There have also been legal differences. According to the European Convention on Human Rights, European countries cannot extradite suspects to countries with the death penalty, and some countries have refused to send anyone to U.S. military tribunals.[279] Even Britain, the strongest U.S. ally in the war on terrorism, refused to extradite two suspects because of lack of evidence.[280] The United States, meanwhile, has unsigned the International Criminal Court treaty and has promised to go to extraordinary measures to prevent U.S. soldiers from being tried for war crimes at the Hague. We won't send our soldiers; they won't send their suspects.

RUSSIA AND CHINA

Whatever their grumbles about relative powerlessness, the Europeans represent an economic counterforce to the United States. Russia and China, meanwhile, have less leverage with the United States, and their geopolitical influence is largely restricted to their own immediate regions and to "rogue" countries that lie outside the U.S. orbit. In this context, both countries have responded shrewdly to the challenges of September 11.

For Russia, after nearly a decade of suffering international criticisms of its war against Chechen separatists, September 11 was a political opportunity to subsume its civil conflicts and ongoing efforts to topple the hated Taliban in the larger "war on terrorism." In other regards, though, Russia's much vaunted cooperation with the United States has been much more grudging. Dealt a weak hand in the aftermath of the Cold War, Russia is struggling to save face in its dealings with the United States. After much protest

	The Views from Europe:			
	Europeans Believe U.S. Foreign Policy			
	Contributed to 9-11			

	France	Germany	Great Britain	Italy
Agree American Foreign Policy Contributed to the September 11 Attacks	63%	52%	57%	51%

Source: The German Marshall Fund of the United States and The Chicago Council on Foreign Relations, "Worldviews 2002," August 2002. Available online at: www.worldviews.org

and the winning of minor concessions, Russia bid farewell to the Anti-Ballistic Missile Treaty, tacitly accepted the U.S. development of missile defense, allowed NATO to expand into its sphere of influence, and even permitted U.S. bases in what had once been the Soviet Union.

But the days of Boris Yeltsin, the drunken heir to Peter the Great's line of Westernizers, are over. Eurasianism, a doctrine whereby Russia turns to the East for inspiration (*ex oriente lux*), is filling the void in Russian foreign policy created by disenchantment with the United States. It is no surprise, then, that Russian President Vladimir Putin pointedly reached out to each member of the "axis of evil" in turn: negotiating a deal on nuclear energy with Iran, consolidating trade deals with Iraq (Russian oil companies controlled 40 percent of Iraqi exports in the UN's oil-for-food program),[281] and meeting with the North Korean leader Kim Jong Il, whom Bush has referred to as a "pygmy" and a "spoiled child at the dinner table."[282] In the absence of an equal partnership with the United States, Russia is covering its bets.

Like Russia, China has used the "war on terrorism" to settle some of its own accounts but has been much freer in its designation of "terrorist." The Chinese leadership has cast its net over not only separatists in Xinjiang, who have indeed resorted to violence on behalf of their cause, but also political dissidents, the generally peaceful Tibetans, and even the pesky believers in the spiritual sect Falun Gong. On the other hand, China has been happy neither with the Bush administration's fixation on its growing military nor with the enhanced flow of U.S. weaponry to Taiwan. And for reasons of trade and, in the case of North Korea, lingering fraternal bonds, China has also maintained good relations with the "axis of evil."

Russia and China are two strong but oppositely charged particles, and it takes a great force to push them together. In the 1950s, this force was Communism, and the entente didn't last long. Four decades on, concerns over U.S. hegemony pushed the two countries to form the Shanghai Cooperation Organization. Both are worried about U.S. encroachment in Central Asia, the capacity that missile defense has in theory to render their nuclear arsenals obsolete, and the Bush administration's predilection for regime change. For the moment, Russia and China find a shallow alliance with the United States to their benefit; if pushed too hard by the winds of unilateralism, they may stop bending and begin pushing back.

THE REST OF THE WORLD

From a dispassionate perspective, the most important aspect about September 11 is not that America suffered an attack or that extremists targeted "Western civilization" but that a transnational group attacked a state in the international system. Viewed from this angle, the reaction of states around the world has not been surprising. Whatever beef they might have had with the United States, other countries understood the threat that a global, transnational terrorist network poses to *all* states. Al-Qaeda challenges the very definition of the state as holder of a monopoly on organized violence. So it is no irony at all that Sudanese leader Omar al-Bashir, previously no champion of American values, has cooperated with the United States on counterterrorism and suppressed anti-American demonstrations on the streets of Khartoum.

As the previous chapters amply demonstrate, politicians the world over acknowledged the dire threat of global terrorism, then quickly took advantage of September 11 to advance their own states' interests. Authoritarian leaders in Central Asia traded their strategic support for U.S. military and economic aid that was free of accompanying demands for democratic change. Colombia and the Philippines took advantage of the changed geopolitical climate to prosecute their own civil wars more harshly. Countries as diverse as Azerbaijan, Djibouti, and Ecuador lined up to receive military handouts from the Pentagon. Regardless of how much U.S. unilateralism rubbed countries the wrong way, they were not above taking advantage of the new dispensation.

The "with us or against us" approach that the Bush administration adopted after September 11 could be understood in both narrow terms (everyone was with us except a handful of "rogues" such as the Taliban and Iraq) or in much broader, civilizational terms. Although he took pains to reach out to Muslims in the United States and Muslim countries for the war in Afghanistan, Bush has increasingly sounded themes of the good West versus the evil rest. The war in Iraq is a case in point. Arab countries, many of whom are no friends of Saddam Hussein, nonetheless drew together against U.S. plans. In September 2002, chief of the Arab League, Amr Moussa, warned the United States that "the gates of Hell will open" if the United States attacks Iraq, and this threat may well prove prophetic in months and years to come.[283] According to the laws of theopolitics, jihad from Washington encourages equal but opposite jihads elsewhere.

The most effective voice for developing countries continues to be the United Nations, despite all of its shortcomings.
Although the UN expressed its sorrow after September 11
and did not stand in the way of the war against Afghanistan,
it has taken a much dimmer view of subsequent U.S. actions.
UN Secretary General Kofi Annan has expended much
effort to avert a war with Iraq and, where possible, to temper
U.S. ambitions. He also tried to remind the United States
that the war on terrorism was not the only global priority. In
his end-of-the-year address in December 2001, Annan pointed out that "[f]or many people in the world 2001 was not
different from 2000 or 1999. It was just another year of living with HIV/AIDS, or in a refugee camp, or under repressive rule, or with crushing poverty."[284]

Popular movements are pushing governments to challenge the Bush administration's power trip. Shortly after
September 11, antiwar protests throughout Europe brought
twenty thousand people into the streets of London, fifteen
thousand in Berlin, and several hundred thousand
marchers between the Italian cities of Perugia and Assisi. In
the United States, meanwhile, several hundred thousand
people marched against Bush policies in Washington, D.C.,
San Francisco, and other cities in April and October 2002,
and again in January 2003. In February, the largest single
day of antiwar demonstrations in history took place in
London, New York, Rome, Sydney, Paris, Barcelona,
Damascus, Berlin, Dublin, Jakarta, and other cities. The
turnout was made more impressive by the fact that protestors were hitting the streets in the millions before the war
officially started. As of March 2003, however, despite rising
anger at home and abroad about the Bush administration's
single-minded pursuit of regime change in Iraq, the protests
have not seemed to affect policy making in Washington.

The global economic justice movement, meanwhile, has

continued strong, despite an initial pause after September 11. While the protests in Calgary around the G8 summit in 2002 managed only three thousand protestors, compared to two hundred thousand the year before in Genoa, anti-globalization protests brought out eighty thousand in Brussels in December 2001 and nearly two hundred fifty thousand in Barcelona in March 2002. At the World Social Forum in Porto Alegre, Brazil—timed to coincide with the meeting of world political and economic leaders in Davos, Switzerland—attendance swelled from fifteen thousand in 2001 to over fifty thousand in 2002 and attracted the respectful attention of mainstream media such as the *Financial Times.*[285] While not specifically antiwar, the global justice movement has consistently pointed out the perils of U.S. unilateralism and the misallocation of resources for defense rather than human needs.

George W. Bush, like most incoming presidents, enjoyed a honeymoon period in his first months in office when he could use his political capital to push his agenda through Congress. Unlike any other president in American history, Bush received an extraordinary second shot of political capital, this one both domestic and international, after September 11. He used this capital to dislodge the Taliban and scatter al-Qaeda, and then, in a much wider and more expensive bid, to expand this war on terrorism to encompass other long-standing U.S. foreign policy goals. European allies, strategic competitors such as Russia and China, multilateral institutions such as the UN and the Arab League, and finally civic movements are groping for a way to respond to this unilateralism. The criticisms are coalescing into a global chorus. The question remains whether any of these criticisms—or the alternatives that follow in the next chapter—will penetrate the Bush administration in what Jean-Marie Colombani so aptly described as the solitude of its power.

CHAPTER SIX

How Things Should Change

by Miriam Pemberton and John Feffer

A WEEK BEFORE the first anniversary of the September 11 attacks, the heads of state of a hundred countries assembled in Johannesburg for the UN World Summit on Sustainable Development. They gathered to accelerate efforts to raise living standards around the world without destroying the global environment in the process, a plan established a decade ago at the historic Earth Summit in Rio de Janeiro.

In symbolic gestures—an empty chair and pair of shoes planted at one session, a sea of buttons asking "Where Is W?"—delegates in Johannesburg noted the conspicuous absence of the U.S. president. Unlike his father ten years before, George W. Bush skipped the summit and sent his secretary of state as his designated hitter. Bush's boycott was supported by a collection of oil companies, including megagiant Exxon Mobil, who wrote the president congratulating him on his good judgment.[286] Petroleum, after all, is a major driving force behind unsustainable development (otherwise known generically as "business as usual").

Colin Powell arrived on the summit's last day, during an impassioned speech by the Palestinian environment minister describing the environmental devastation wreaked by the Israeli occupation. The U.S. secretary of state could be seen chatting with the minister next to him, his translation earphones on the table by his side. Powell's schedule at the summit focused not on sustainable development but on behind-the-scenes lobbying to convince the assembled leaders to back U.S. plans to attack Iraq. The United States had clearly come to lecture, not to listen.

Indeed, the United States has been suffering gradual hearing loss for some time. The louder the world raises its objections, the more deafly the United States soldiers on. The historical moment created by the September 11 attacks could have accomplished a minor medical miracle by restoring to the United States the ability to hear. In fact, the American government and the American people gratefully listened to the expressions of sympathy that came pouring in from around the world and were surprised to hear from some unexpected quarters such as Libya's Muammar Qaddafi and Cuba's Fidel Castro. But the restoration of hearing was only partial. Our leaders still could not hear *why* so much of the world is unhappy with U.S. foreign policy. They could hear the sweet strains of sympathy but not the bass rumblings of dissatisfaction.

The United States needs to listen for two reasons: our allies and our adversaries. The challenge of international terrorism clearly requires international cooperation, so the United States must listen to allies. Listening is central to the practice of multilateralism. Multilateralism, like politics, is the art of the possible, and this art is practiced through conversation. Instead, the Bush administration has pressured allies to back the wider "war on terrorism" and ignored the multilateral treaties that our allies support. The U.S. government has also undermined our allies' diplomatic overtures. European countries are engaging Iran. Japanese Prime Minister Junichiro Koizumi shook hands with North Korea's Kim Jong Il in a historic September 2002 summit, and South Korea is currently urging a peaceful resolution to the nuclear crisis on the Korean peninsula. Our allies in the UN worked hard to avert war with Iraq. Virtually every state views terrorism as a threat to its existence, but most ongoing resolutions (in Ireland, in Spain) are being negotiated, not imposed by force of arms. Coalition-building among our allies requires greater acknowledgment of their strengths, experiences, and concerns. If the U.S. government abandons the fundamentals of diplomatic engagement, U.S. allies such as Israel and Colombia will be even less likely to alter their own hard-line policies.

With our adversaries—actual, potential, or imagined—listening is also critical. Popular opposition to U.S. policies is rising around the globe. Again the Earth Summit was symbolic: Secretary Powell's speech could barely be delivered over the loud and recurrent chorus of disapproval. The unilateralism of the Bush administration—so dramatically recounted in the previous chapters, crystallized in "The National Security Strategy of the United States" released in September 2002, and implemented most recently in the war in Iraq—has been the exact opposite of a dialogue, and this marks a dramatic change in how the United States conducts foreign policy. Our present leaders have graduated from the take-it-or-leave-it school of diplomacy. This is the art of the impossible, a mafioso's take on democracy, and this is the art that the United States practiced so deafly at the World Summit on Sustainable Development: nonattendance, nonengagement, nonnegotiation.

Listening is not a substitute for action. The United States must indeed respond to the threat of international terrorism. In the short term, the United States has no choice but to fortify its vulnerable infrastructure—its cyber networks, its intelligence apparatus, its utilities—against terrorist attack. But it also has no choice but to resist the intoxicating effects of its largely unchecked power. The challenge—for the people of the United States and for the people of the world—is how to coax, prod, persuade, and perhaps even force the Bush administration back into the world of politics, into the world of the possible, into a world in which the superpower listens and not simply lectures. The following modest suggestions are aimed at carving out a more modest role for the United States. They all hinge on one thing: changing the terms of U.S. engagement with the world and transforming the United States into a responsible international partner.

This transformation can be expressed in language that directly appeals to the Bush administration. In its relationship with the world, the United States should be both compassionate and conservative. Compassion literally means "to suffer with." A compassionate policy would marry empathy to geopolitics in an effort to address the problems of those suffering from debt, disease, and despair around the world. A conservative policy, meanwhile, is one that recognizes limits—the limits of law, tradition, the environment, and, indeed, the power of the United States itself. It is time to reclaim these honorable words—compassion, conservative—from a U.S. administration that is neither.

RECOGNIZING LIMITS

The militarism that lies at the heart of the U.S. power trip is fundamentally different from the Cold War version. The Soviet Union—and Soviet nuclear weapons—established certain hard constraints that defined U.S. military policy. During the Cold War, the United States did not use nuclear weapons (though it considered doing so), nor did it directly attack the Soviet Union or China. Pentagon strategists conformed to a relatively conservative balance-of-power approach to geopolitics. Those who have fought in wars know very well the limits of military action. It is not surprising that some of the key opponents of Bush's plan to attack Iraq were generals such as Anthony Zinni, Brent Scowcroft, and Norman Schwarzkopf.

But the hawks in the Bush administration—Dick Cheney, Donald Rumsfeld, Paul Wolfowitz—are anything but conservative. They have pushed at the very limits of traditional military doctrine: embracing preemptive strikes, contemplating the use of nuclear weapons in warfare, violating long-standing arms control treaties, and spreading weapons everywhere from Uzbekistan to outer space. There is a dangerous liberality in these policies. Weapons are being given away liberally; arms control treaties are being interpreted liberally. This liberality verges on the libertine: the United States is acting without moral restraint in its military policy.

This inability to act with restraint extends to the field of resources. The American addiction to petroleum propels our policies in the Middle East and justifies the expansion of U.S. military operations into West Africa, Central Asia, and Latin America. The more oil we burn, the more oil we need, and neither arctic wilderness nor human rights abroad has interfered with getting our fix. The Bush administration's ties to Big Oil, "just say yes" approach to increased oil consumption, and reluctance to redirect U.S. policy toward renewable energy sources have made a bad situation considerably worse.

A properly conservative U.S. policy would recognize the importance of limits, controlling and reducing weapons of mass destruction, reducing rather than distributing arms, cutting back on the number of military bases, and acknowledging the lessons of history to circumscribe military campaigns around the world. Likewise, Americans must either recognize the limits imposed by the environment—resource depletion, ozone disappearance—or the environment will simply impose those limits by itself. Our liberal use of gasoline in sports utility vehicles and our liberal misuse of other resources such as food and water far exceed the portion allotted to us by our percentage of the global population.[287] In this sense, liberal is indeed a dirty word.

Terrorism, too, is a doctrine that ignores limits. Terrorists violate the greatest military taboo by targeting not soldiers but civilians. Yet this is not the monopoly of terrorists. In World War II, the Germans bombed London, the Americans bombed Dresden and Hiroshima, the Japanese slaughtered civilians in China and elsewhere in Asia. Nuclear warfare is fundamentally a terrorist operation, for it kills noncombatants. The "war on terrorism," then, is a misnomer, for it suggests that the two elements in the equation are distinct. It is time to strip the terrorist elements from modern warfare and impose conservative constraints on military operations. A war on terrorism that threatens to become permanent and all-encompassing will dissolve all international laws and lead the world into a downward spiral of all against all. The braided rope of militarism, oil dependency, and the war on terrorism that currently binds U.S. foreign policy so tightly is certainly difficult to cut. Conservation in its literal sense is where to begin. The U.S. government must conserve existing arms control treaties (on testing, proliferation, and so on), conserve natural resources, and take a conservative approach to terrorism that relies more on the established mechanisms of law enforcement than on the latest instruments of war.

EXERCISING COMPASSION

According to polls, Americans believe that foreign aid constitutes roughly 20 percent of the federal budget.[288] This is an intriguing myth, for it assumes that the United States already has a compassionate policy. Anti-Americanism, whether expressed by terrorists or hecklers at the Johannesburg meeting, then appears to be rank ingratitude. Yet in fact the United States provides less in foreign aid (as a percentage of GNP) than any other industrialized nation: a mere sliver of one percent.

Increasing foreign aid is an integral part of a compassionate policy. But aid must not only be significantly increased, it must be transformed. In distributing economic aid, the United States tends to reward allies rather than address the poorest of the poor. The aid comes with strings attached: countries have to embrace the neoliberal model of structural adjustment, 80 percent of the aid requires purchases from U.S. companies, and the majority of the aid is military. A hungry child knows neither politics nor economics, to update Ronald Reagan's famous dictum, and these strings do not help the hungry.

A February 2002 Senate resolution asserted that since "poverty, hunger, political uncertainty, and social instability are the principal causes of violence and conflict around the world," U.S. foreign assistance programs "should play an increased role in the global fight against terrorism [by providing] increased financial assistance to countries with impoverished and disadvantaged populations that are the breeding grounds for terrorism."[289] Strictly speaking, in aiming to prevent future attacks against the United States, foreign aid of this sort is more a matter of self-interest than compassion. But the global need is so dire that the rationale for increased aid is less important than the increase itself. The United States must start with debt cancellation, as well as adhering to its promises to provide $700 million for the Heavily Indebted Poor Countries Initiative. Staggering debt payments are perhaps the single largest obstacle preventing poor and middle-ranking countries from crossing the development gap. Demilitarizing aid and focusing on the poorest of the poor, key elements of any compassionate policy, will alleviate suffering more fairly than the current system of rewarding strategic allies.

Under the banner of free trade, the United States has been negotiating trade agreements in order to engineer the balance of power to its own benefit. It has been busily trying to fix the rules, in other words, to make trade another tool of U.S. "power projection." Rescuing trade from its dubious "free" variation requires a certain injection of compassion into the process. "Free" trade has caused considerable suffering in the world—poorly paid labor in Mexican maquiladoras, hazardous working conditions in Chinese sweatshops, bankrupt farmers throughout the developing world. The United States must sign the remaining core labor standards promoted by the International Labor Organization (ILO) and pressure other countries to do so as well. Acknowledging that our prosperity was built on a foundation of protected national industries, we must allow other countries to build up their own productive enterprises. To create the conditions in which workers can organize safer workplaces and countries can find ways to participate in the world economic system on an equal footing, the United States must also establish limits on speculative investments and help reform international financial institutions so that they adhere to their original purpose of closing the gap between the developing countries and the industrialized world.

A NEW ENGAGEMENT WITH THE WORLD

The Bush administration espouses "compassionate conservatism" but does not practice what it preaches. Echoing back the administration's words will not necessarily trigger a conversion, particularly since listening has proven not to be the strong suit of those currently in power in Washington. To check the administration's power trip, there must be an equal counterforce. Some of this force will be provided by the sheer outrage of the outside world. Many European governments are aghast at the U.S. government's refusal to play by the rules of the game. The Chinese and the Russians have grudgingly and perhaps only temporarily acceded to U.S. demands. The Arab world is demanding a more balanced approach to the stand-off between Israel and Palestine. The UN, told to go to the back of the bus, is uncomfortable with the United States climbing into the driver's seat.

The rest of the counterforce, however, must come from within. In the United States itself, the American public has been hesitant about expanding the war on terrorism beyond a narrow focus on those responsible for September 11.[290] The democratic process, which took such a beating in Florida in December 2000, still holds much promise, although congressional opposition to the Bush agenda has been less a matter of collective action than individual conscience—Barbara Lee's (D-CA) solitary vote against going to war in Afghanistan, Russell Feingold's (D-WI) solitary vote against the U.S.A. PATRIOT Act. While certain politicians have taken courageous stands, other elected representatives will require more "street heat"—pressure from concerned constituents—particularly after the 2002 elections returned control of both houses of Congress to the Republican Party.

During the last efflorescence of U.S. unilateralism in the Reagan years, powerful social movements helped to prevent the worst-case scenarios. The peace movement pressured the Reagan administration to negotiate with the Soviet Union on nuclear missile withdrawals from Europe and reductions in strategic arsenals. The anti-intervention movement helped deter a direct U.S. invasion of El Salvador and Nicaragua. The antiapartheid movement helped to dissolve U.S. support for the South African regime.

Today, the global justice movement and the peace movement are similarly countering U.S. policies around the world. The global justice movement has had extraordinary successes exposing the defects of structural adjustment models and changing the terms of debate on debt and local control. As the war on terrorism and the war on Iraq absorb national attention, this momentum has slowed but not stopped. The peace movement meanwhile has forged transnational ties in an effort to substitute robust multilateralism for rash unilateralism. Such international cooperation is the proper antidote to the U.S. military and economic power trip. But effective resistance will require cooperation not only across borders but across topics as well: the global justice and the peace movements need to forge a common critique and establish a common agenda for action.

The nonviolent end of the Cold War—forty years of military alert ending with hardly a shot fired—created an opportunity for the world to find its way to an order based less on power balances than on genuine international cooperation. So far this has been largely an opportunity missed. The September 11 attacks were a tragic reminder of the imperative for the United States to redirect its energies away from the pursuit of unchallengeable economic and military power. The United States cannot ask the rest of the world to join in its war on terrorism while dismissing all other initiatives for international cooperation. More important, problems such as the proliferation of weapons of mass destruction and global warming require immediate, urgent, concerted action.

In 1935, the international order faced a dire threat. Fascism, as a doctrine, set itself against a democratic, multilateral system. But the precipitating factor for the demise of the League of Nations—the predecessor to the United Nations—was Italy's invasion of Abyssinia in that year. International norms could not survive this final violation.

Seventy years later, a considerably stronger international community faces a similar problem, though the threat itself has bifurcated. Whatever challenge terrorism poses to the current democratic, multilateral system, it is the ostensibly democratic United States, in its unilateral attempt to remake the world in its own image, that more directly threatens the United Nations and the rule of international law.[291] How many U.S.-led invasions will it take before the UN follows the League of Nations into history's dustbin?

As the signs at railway crossings once advised motorists, the United States must "stop, look, and listen." To do otherwise is to court disaster. After the Bush administration stops and listens—or is forced to do so by domestic pressures and the international community—we can begin the discussion of how things really should change.

Afterword

by Susan F. Hirsch

IN LATE AUGUST 1998, just thirteen days after two of its embassies were bombed in East Africa, the U.S. government ordered Tomahawk missile strikes on targets in Khartoum, Sudan, and Khost, Afghanistan. With investigations ongoing, the missiles pronounced a quick verdict and delivered destructive retaliation for the embassy bombings, which killed over two hundred people, including twelve Americans, and injured five thousand, mostly Africans. The United States officially described the missile strikes as "self-defense" to destroy the potential for terrorists to plan or execute future attacks from these sites.[292] Extensive damage, injuries, and deaths resulted from the strikes in Afghanistan; in Sudan, where a pharmaceutical plant was destroyed, no deaths were reported. The U.S. government has never released detailed analyses of these strikes.

The bombing of the U.S. embassy in Dar es Salaam, Tanzania—a horrific act of political violence—was a personal tragedy for me. The blast killed my husband, Abdulrahman Abdallah, who was waiting near the embassy entrance while I ran an errand inside. As a surviving victim, though, I was deeply distressed by the retaliatory missile strikes, which I considered to be yet more acts of violence in a confusing and destructive conflict that could only worsen. Just as I was struggling to comprehend the geopolitics that led to my personal tragedy, the missile strikes by my own government seemed to foreclose inquiry into who was responsible for the bombings and why they had attacked these U.S.

targets. Moreover, I worried that the U.S. military's show of force would further inflame anger against the United States in many parts of the world. Despite emphasis on their role as preventing future attacks, the strikes were also depicted as a just response to avenge the suffering of "innocent victims."[293] As Secretary of State Madeleine Albright claimed at the time, "[W]hen the United States is attacked, when our people are taken out, we will stand out unilaterally in self-defense and really let the world know what we believe in."[294] As controversy swirled about whether the missile strikes had achieved any relevant military or political goals, I became angry that my government had so swiftly resorted to an arrogant display of force that, as the events of September 11 attest, only furthered the resolve of those determined to commit violent acts.[295] As one commentator notes, the missile strikes were a "power" response to terrorism rather than the more common "criminal justice" approach.[296] To the extent that this response was pursued on my behalf as a victim, I reject it completely.

Contributors to this volume have illuminated the varied and extensive "power" moves in foreign policy that have followed in response to the terrorist attacks of the early twenty-first century. The analyses make clear that the quest for unilateral domination—particularly over natural resources and the global economy—has determined the trajectory of certain sectors of the U.S. government for some time. Following September 11, the threat of terrorist enemies close to "home" has provided convenient justification for acting on those long-standing goals. In offering a critical analysis of the major political realignments that display and cement U.S power globally, this volume importantly directs attention to the dangers posed by a foreign policy pursued in narrow self-interest, devoid of an ethical imperative, and sorely needing a commitment to justice.

Current efforts toward U.S. global domination—through military, political, and ideological means—repeat the serious political and moral flaws of previous attempts, although perhaps on a larger scale. I'll mention just two objectionable correlates of U.S. quests for supremacy that focus on the African continent, my area of expertise. First, attempts to dominate are routinely accompanied by a lack of interest in areas of the world not of direct and immediate concern to what the U.S. government perceives to be its economic and strategic goals. Obtaining knowledge about marginalized regions of the world and the people living there holds low priority. For example, in the rush to achieve influence in both the emerging states of the former Soviet Union and the new markets in Asia, U.S. attention toward much of Africa declined in the 1980s and 1990s. Ironically, directing support to fledgling democracies in regions such as Eastern Europe coincided with ignoring human rights and civil liberties violations by virtual dictators in Africa and other regions.

Rather than examining the African continent's political complexities, the United States propped up the likes of Mobutu Sese Seko in Zaire and Daniel arap Moi in Kenya in an effort to maintain stability. As the United States built new embassies in Eastern Europe and Asia, it allowed many in Africa to deteriorate with respect to facilities and security, including those in Dar es Salaam and Nairobi.[297] Disinterest in African nations, and insufficient respect for African people, is a tragic and recurring consequence of policies that put U.S. power and gain before thoughtful, egalitarian connection with other nations, especially the poorest. Unstable and threatening situations are likely to result, as well as strained relations with people and nations that might have been reliable allies. Moreover, the dearth of knowledge means that ossified stereotypes persist. For example, the confrontation of "radical Islam" and "the West" leaves out of the picture large moderate Muslim populations, especially those living throughout Africa.

A second major flaw of U.S. power moves is that they are pursued with little concern for the severe inequalities of current global economic relations. The U.S. drive to dominate proceeds as if unaware of the rising resentment of large segments of the world's population that suffer under crushing debt burdens, crumbling infrastructures, and weakened health and education systems. Disenfranchised people doubtless view power in the face of economic injustice as corrupt and illegitimate. No one should be surprised if they mount, join, or support struggles to bring down that power. For instance, women's organizations, Ogoni liberation groups, and ordinary West African people have long contested the environmental degradation and labor exploitation that Shell and other multinational oil companies are responsible for in Nigeria. Little known to American consumers are their protest tactics, which include sophisticated Internet sites, work stoppages, and a traditional practice whereby women remove their clothes in public to shame those who ignore pleas for relief from oppression. Because they do not touch the lives of most Americans, such inequalities and such protests remain largely invisible to those who pump Nigerian oil into their cars.

After the September 11 attacks, one tactic of U.S. officials seeking popular support for their policies has been to declare that "we are all victims of terrorism" in an attempt to garner public support for the recent projects of dominance, which include limits on civil liberties, xenophobic immigration policies, and aggressive military and political action by the United States worldwide. This invocation of victim status seeks to encourage responses commonly associated with victimhood, such as fear, rage, and the desire for revenge, and attributes to victims a narrow sense of justice as payback for harm inflicted. Victims of terrorism are certainly capable of those responses, especially in the immediate aftermath of a terror attack. But such an emphasis overlooks the more positive and productive approaches to justice that many are capable of advocating in the face of tragedy. More than a few victims counter their own unjust experience of terrorism with a commitment to work for justice in its broadest sense, not as the end product of revenge but as fairness, integrity, and equality. If we are to think of ourselves as victims, then we should focus on the great gains made possible by committed victims working against injustice, including acts of violence and inequality.

Several projects have emerged out of the desire—by victims and others—for justice in this broad sense. For example, many victims of September 11 argued strenuously against the war in Afghanistan, although their voices were muffled by the media emphasis on conventional representations of patriotism. Amber Amundson, whose husband was killed while working at the Pentagon, wrote in a *Chicago Tribune* editorial: "I have heard angry rhetoric by some Americans, including many of our nation's leaders, who advise a heavy dose of revenge and punishment. To those leaders, I would like to make clear that my family and I take no comfort in your words of rage. If you choose to respond to this incomprehensible brutality by perpetuating violence against other innocent human beings, you may not do so in the name of justice for my husband."[298] Some victims and other interested parties traveled to Afghanistan to meet with people who had suffered losses from the U.S. bombing and to share perspectives on violence and hopes for peace. Those who made this visit have helped to pressure the U.S. Congress to compensate Afghani civilian victims.[299]

My own experience as a victim has led me to advocate that

the U.S. government deal with terrorist acts through the criminal justice system. This approach seeks to avoid both the violence of U.S. military action and the violations of equal protection that military tribunals will likely produce. Turning to law, however, requires vigilance to ensure that the legal process is as fair as possible. My participation in the embassy bombings trial in 2001 confirmed that in trials of accused terrorists, the potential for injustice—prejudice against the defendants, misuse of classified information—presents a grave challenge to the U.S. legal system. As a result of the trial, four men face life in prison. Limited media coverage, combined with the prosecution's refusal to acknowledge the political goals behind the bombings, meant that we missed an opportunity to reflect on the nature of the threat posed by al-Qaeda. Another unjust consequence of the American legal system is the death penalty. Bud Welch, who lost his daughter in the 1995 Oklahoma City bombing, has spoken out against the death penalty, including for convicted perpetrator Timothy McVeigh. Noting the U.S. government's shortcomings in legal approaches to terrorism, France and other nations have refused to cooperate with some prosecutions. The U.S. government's stubborn refusal to participate in the new International Criminal Court is another example of misguided unilateralism. Attempting to stand alone and above other nations, the United States risks an isolation it can ill afford.

Finally, the family of Daniel Pearl, a journalist killed in Pakistan while covering the aftermath of the Afghanistan conflict, provides an example of how those who have suffered can work productively for justice. The foundation created in Daniel's name promotes the goals behind his work, which include "uncompromised objectivity and integrity; insightful and unconventional perspective; tolerance and respect for people of all cultures; unshaken belief in the effectiveness of education and communication...."[300]

The pursuit and dissemination of knowledge, particularly about areas remote from the United States and yet dramatically affected by its policies, would aid in exposing the injustice of current political and economic conditions.

As this volume demonstrates, a candid discussion of the U.S. role worldwide requires considerable attention to the global economic inequality that U.S. foreign policy exacerbates. Many people and groups worldwide are working for global economic justice. The goals and commitments motivating these groups serve as counterpoints to current U.S. goals, which amount to little more than military and political support for economic expansion, ultimately benefiting only a few. By offering a strong critique of unilateralism and other perils of U.S. foreign policy, this book has illuminated other avenues toward justice and away from the dangerous and isolating path the United States is currently pursuing. As the first Tanzanian president, Julius Nyerere, said in 1996, "Each of us, as individuals, as 'workers by hand or by brain,' and as leaders, has the responsibility to act against the oppressions of poverty, ignorance, and disease.... Neither public recognition nor lack of it provides an excuse for slackening our efforts. Without violence or hatred, we must work for a world where all human beings can live in peace and justice."[301]

U.S. List of Foreign Terrorist Organizations

1. Abu Nidal Organization (ANO)—Iraq, also present in the Bekaa Valley of Lebanon as well as in several refugee camps along the coast of Lebanon. Limited presence in Sudan and Syria.

2. Abu Sayyaf Group—Philippines and has expanded its operations to Malaysia.

3. Al-Aqsa Martyrs Brigade—West Bank and Israel and the Gaza strip.

4. Armed Islamic Group—Algeria.

5. Asbat al-Ansar—Southern Lebanon.

6. Aum Shinrikyo—Operates in Japan but is present in Australia, Russian, UK, Germany Taiwan, Sri Lanka, former Yugoslavia, and the U.S.

7. Basque Fatherland and Liberty (ETA)—Northern Spain and southwestern France.

8. Gama'a al-Islamiyya (Islamic Group)—Egypt but also has a presence in Sudan, United Kingdom, Afghanistan, Austria, and Yemen.

9. HAMAS (Islamic Resistance Movement)—Israel and West Bank settlements.

10. Harakat ul-Mujahidin (HUM)—Pakistan but conducts attacks mainly in Kashmir.

11. Hizballah—Lebanon, conducts operations in the West Bank and Israel and the Gaza strip.

12. Islamic Movement of Uzbekistan—Based in Tajikistan and Afghanistan but operates in Uzbekistan, Afghanistan, Kyrgyzstan, and Tajikistan.

13. Jaish-e-Mohammed (JEM) (Army of Mohammed)—Pakistan, but conduct attacks mainly in Kashmir.

14. al-Jihad (Egyptian Islamic Jihad)—Egypt, but is present in Yemen, Afghanistan, Pakistan, Sudan, Lebanon, and United Kingdom.

15. Kahane Chai (Kach)—Israel and West Bank settlements.

16. Kurdistan Worker's Party (PKK)—Turkey, Europe, and the Middle East.

17. Lashkar-e Tayyiba (LT) (Army of the Righteous)—Pakistan.

18. Lashkar i Jhangvi—Pakistan.

19. Liberation Tigers of Tamil Eelam (LTTE)—Sri Lanka.

20. Mujahedin-e Khalq Organization (MEK)—Based in Iran but holds an extensive overseas network.

21. National Liberation Army (ELN)—Colombia and the southwest Colombia-Venezuela border.

22. Palestinian Islamic Jihad (PIJ)—Headquartered in Syria. Actions primarily in Israel and to a lesser degree in Jordan and Lebanon.

23. Palestinian Liberation Front—Originally based in Tunisia but currently located in Iraq.

24. Popular Front for the Liberation of Palestine General Command (PFLP-GC)—Headquartered in Syria. Active against Israel from camps based in Lebanon.

25. PFLP-General Command—Southern Lebanon and various parts of the Middle East and Western Europe.

26. al-Qaida—Key officials reside or have been known to reside in Afghanistan. The operation has a worldwide network in a number of countries.

27. Real IRA—Northern Ireland, Republic of Ireland, and other areas of Great Britain.

28. Revolutionary Armed Forces of Colombia (FARC)—Colombia with some activity in Venezuela, Panama, and Ecuador.

29. Revolutionary Nuclei (formerly ELA)—Athens, Greece.

30. Revolutionary Organization 17 November—Athens, Greece.

31. Revolutionary People's Liberation Army/Front (DHKP/C)—Turkey.

32. Salafist Group for Call and Combat (GSPC)—Algeria.

33. Shining Path (Sendero Luminoso)—Peru.

34. United Self-Defense Forces of Colombia (AUC)—Colombia.

35. Communist Party of the Philippines/New People's Army (CPP/NPA)—Philippines.

36. Jemaah Islamiya Organization (JI)—Southeast Asia.

Sources: Department of State, "Fact Sheet: Foreign Terrorist Organizations," January 30, 2003. Available online at: http://www.state.gov/s/ct/rls/fs/2003/17067.htm; Department of State, "Patterns of Global Terrorism, 2000," April 2001. Available online at: http://library.nps.navy.mil/home/tgp/tgpndx.htm; The International Policy Institute for Counter-Terrorism, "Terrorist Organization Profiles," 2002. Available online at: www.ict.org.il.

The Project for the New American Century

Signatories of 1997 Statement of Principles

Elliott Abrams
• National Security Council Senior Director for Democracy, Human Rights, and International Operations
• Former Assistant Secretary of State for Human Rights and for Inter-American Affairs in Reagan administration

Gary Bauer
• 1999-2000: Republican presidential candidate
• 1989-99: Founder and President, Family Research Council
• Director, White House Office of Policy Development in Reagan administration

William J. Bennett
• Codirector, Empower America; Chairman, Americans for Victory Over Terrorism
• Distinguished Fellow, Heritage Foundation
• Director, White House Office of Drug Control Policy in Bush Sr. administration
• Secretary of Education in Reagan administration

Jeb Bush
• Governor, State of Florida

Richard B. Cheney
• Vice President to George W. Bush
• 1989-Jan. 1993: Secretary of Defense
• 1975-77: White House Chief of Staff

Eliot A. Cohen
• Professor and Director of Strategic Studies, The Paul H. Nitze School of Advanced International Studies
• Policy planning staff of the Department of Defense in Bush Sr. administration

Midge Decter
- Board of Trustees of the Heritage Foundation
- Executive Director of the Committee for a Free World in Reagan administration
- Founder of Coalition for a Democratic Majority in 1970s

Paula Dobriansky
- Undersecretary of State for Global Affairs
- Office of European and Soviet Affairs at the National Security Council in Reagan administration

Steve Forbes
- President and CEO of Forbes magazine
- 1996 and 2000: Campaigned for Republican presidential nomination

Aaron Friedberg
- Henry Alfred Kissinger Chair in Foreign Policy and International Relations at the Library of Congress
- Consultant to the National Security Council in Reagan administration

Francis Fukuyama
- Bernard Schwartz Professor of International Political Economy at The Paul H. Nitze School of Advanced International Studies, The Johns Hopkins University
- State Department Policy Planning Staff in Bush Sr. administration
- Author: The End of History and the Last Man (1992)

Frank Gaffney
- CEO of Center for Security Policy
- Assistant Secretary of Defense for International Security Policy in Reagan administration

Fred C. Ikle
- Senior scholar at the Center for Strategic and International Studies
- Undersecretary of Defense for Policy in Reagan administration
- 1973-77: Director of the Arms Control and Disarmament Agency in Nixon and Ford administrations

Donald Kagan
- Professor of History and Classics, Yale University

Zalmay Khalilzad
- U.S. Special Envoy to Afghanistan
- Special Assistant to the President and Senior Director for Gulf, Southwest Asia, and other Regional Issues, National Security Council
- Deputy Undersecretary of Defense for Policy Planning in Bush Sr. administration
- State Department Policy Planning Staff in Reagan administration

I. Lewis Libby
- Chief of Staff to Vice President Dick Cheney
- Assistant to the Vice President for National Security Affairs
- 1998: Legal Adviser to the U.S. House of Representatives' Select Committee on U.S. National Security and Military/Commercial Concerns with the Peoples' Republic of China, commonly known as the "Cox Committee"
- 1989-93: Deputy Undersecretary of Defense for Policy

Norman Podhoretz
- Senior Fellow, Hudson Institute
- 1960-95: Editor in Chief, Commentary magazine

Dan Quayle
- 1989-93: U.S. Vice President
- 1980-89: U.S. Senator from Indiana

Peter W. Rodman
- Assistant Secretary of Defense for International Security Affairs
- State Department Policy Planning Staff in Reagan administration

Stephen P. Rosen
- Director, Olin Institute of Strategic Studies at Harvard University and Professor of National Security and Military Affairs at Harvard

Henry S. Rowen
- Senior Fellow, Hoover Institution
- Director, Stanford University's Asia/Pacific Research Center
- Assistant Secretary of Defense for International Security Affairs in the Ford and Bush Sr. administrations

Donald Rumsfeld
- Secretary of Defense
- 1998-99: Chairman of the U.S. Government Commission to Assess the Ballistic Missile Threat to the United States

Vin Weber
- Chairman of the Board of Directors, National Endowment for Democracy
- Vice Chairman of Empower America
- 1981-93: U.S. House of Representatives member from Minnesota

George Weigel
- John M. Olin Chair in Religion and American Democracy at Ethics and Public Policy Center
- Former President, Ethics and Public Policy Center
- Author: Witness to Hope: The Biography of John Paul II (1997)

Paul Dundes Wolfowitz
- Deputy Secretary of Defense
- 1994-2001: Dean of The Paul H. Nitze School of Advanced International Studies, The Johns Hopkins University
- Undersecretary of Defense for Policy in Bush Sr. administration
- U.S. Ambassador to the Republic of Indonesia, Assistant Secretary of State for East Asian and Pacific Affairs, Department of State, and Director of Policy Planning for the Department of State in Reagan administration

Other PNAC Principals

Bruce P. Jackson
- Project Director, Project for the New American Century
- Member of Board of Advisors of the Center for Security Policy
- Vice President, Strategy and Planning, Corporate Strategic Development for the Lockheed Martin Corporation
- 2000: Chairman for Republican Party platform's subcommittee on National Security and Foreign Policy
- 1997-99: Director, Global Development for Lockheed Martin Corporation

Reuel Marc Gerecht
- Director of the Middle East Initiative, Project for the New American Century
- Resident Fellow and Scholar, American Enterprise Institute
- 1985-94: Middle Eastern Specialist, Central Intelligence Agency

Robert Kagan
- Cofounder and Project Director, Project for the New American Century
- Contributing editor at *The Weekly Standard*
- Department of State: Deputy for Policy, Bureau of Inter-American Affairs and principal speechwriter for Secretary of State in Reagan administration

Jeane Kirkpatrick
- Senior Fellow, Scholar, and Director of Foreign and Defense Policy Studies, American Enterprise Institute
- Codirector of Empower America
- 1981-85: U.S. Representative to the United Nations

William Kristol
- Cofounder and Chairman of the Project for the New American Century
- Editor and publisher of *The Weekly Standard*
- Chief of Staff to Vice President Dan Quayle
- Chief of Staff to Secretary of Education William Bennett in Reagan administration

Richard Perle
- Resident Fellow, American Enterprise Institute
- Chairman, Defense Policy Board, Department of Defense
- Assistant Secretary of Defense for International Security Policy in Reagan administration

R. James Woolsey
- Partner at the law firm of Shea & Gardner in Washington, DC
- 1999-2000: member of National Commission on Terrorism
- 1998: Commission to Assess the Ballistic Missile Threat to the U.S. (Rumsfeld Commission)
- 1993-95: Director of the Central Intelligence Agency
- Undersecretary of the Navy in Carter administration

Source: Tom Barry and Jim Lobe, "U.S. Foreign Policy—Attention, Right Face, Forward March," *Foreign Policy In Focus, Special Report,* April 2002. Available online at: http://www.fpif.org/papers/02right/index.html.

Americans for Victory Over Terrorism

William J. Bennett*
(see Appendix B)

William P. Barr
- U.S. Attorney General in Bush. Sr. administration
- Deputy Assistant for legal policy at Reagan White House
- Asst. legislative counsel at CIA in 1977

Frank Gaffney
(see Appendix B)

Lawrence Kadish
- Founding chairman, Committee for Security and Peace in the Middle East
- Chairman, Republican Jewish Coalition

Walid Phares
- Professor, Florida Atlantic University
- Author, numerous books on Middle East

Ruth Wise
- Professor, Harvard University
- Author: *If I Am Not Myself: The Liberal Betrayal of the Jews*

R. James Woolsey
(see Appendix B)

* Bennett is AVOT's chairman, and others are AVOT's senior advisers.

Source: Jim Lobe, "War on Dissent Widens," *Foreign Policy In Focus,* March 15, 2002. Available online at: http://www.fpif.org/commentary/2002/0203avot_body.html.

Going It Alone

Abandoning the Multilateral Framework

MAJOR ARMS CONTROL TREATIES

ANTI-BALLISTIC MISSILE TREATY

The ABM treaty prohibited nationwide anti-ballistic missile defenses, limiting each side to two deployment areas (one to defend the national capital and one to defend an ICBM field). On December 13, 2001, President George W. Bush made the historic announcement that the U.S. would withdraw from the 1972 Anti-Ballistic Missile Treaty to pursue deployment of a national missile defense.

BIOLOGICAL WEAPONS CONVENTION

A protocol to strengthen the Biological Weapons Convention of 1972, which bans germ weapons but contains no verification provisions, was close to completion in 2001 when the U.S., alone among the 144 parties to the convention, turned it down and brought the negotiations to a halt. On December 7, 2001, Under Secretary of State for Arms Control John Bolton advocated the termination of the group in charge of negotiating the verification protocol in the midst of dealing with the spread of anthrax through the U.S. postal system.

COMPREHENSIVE TEST BAN TREATY (CTBT)

The CTBT bans all explosive nuclear tests. The U.S. is among the 160 nations that signed the treaty, but ratification of the Test Ban Treaty was defeated by the U.S. Senate in October 1999. Since gaining office, President Bush has stated his opposition to the Treaty, but has said that for the time being the United States would continue the moratorium begun in 1992 on any underground nuclear testing. Key countries that have not ratified include the U.S., China, India, Pakistan, and North Korea.

CONVENTION ON THE PROHIBITION OF LANDMINES

The Convention on the Prohibition of The Use, Stockpiling, Production and Transfer of Anti-Personnel Mines and on Their Destruction was signed in Ottawa on September 18, 1997 and the treaty entered into force on September 17, 1998. Every country in the Western Hemisphere has signed the treaty except the United States and Cuba, and every NATO member has signed except the United States and Turkey. Through the treaty, parties agree to "never use anti-personnel mines" or "produce, otherwise acquire, stockpile, retain, or develop" anti-personnel mines. U.S. military officials attempted to obtain exemptions for mines that could deactivate themselves over time and for the mines along the border between the two Koreas, but neither was accepted. Since entering into office, the Bush administration has rejected the convention.

CHEMICAL WEAPONS CONVENTION (CWC)

While the U.S. has been a member of the CWC since 1997, the U.S. Congress included a series of unilateral exemptions. First, U.S. law allows the president to refuse any inspection in the United States if the President determines that it "may pose a threat" to U.S. national security interests. Second, no samples collected during an inspection can leave U.S. territory for analysis. A third measure narrowed the number of facilities that could be monitored under the convention. If other nations emulated these examples, they could seek to block challenges or other inspections, deny inspectors permission to send chemical samples abroad for detailed analysis at independent laboratories, or decrease considerably the number of facilities worldwide that are open to routine inspection.

MAJOR ENVIRONMENTAL TREATIES

BASEL CONVENTION ON TRANSBOUNDARY MOVEMENTS OF HAZARDOUS WASTES

The Basel Convention on the Control of Transboundary Movements of Hazardous Wastes and their Disposal was adopted in 1989 and entered into force in May 1992. This global environmental treaty strictly regulates international movement of hazardous wastes and obliges its Parties to ensure that such wastes are managed and disposed of in an environmentally sound manner. It also protects the right of states to ban entry of foreign waste within their territories. The Basel Convention was signed by the United States on March 22, 1989, but has not been ratified.

CONVENTION ON BIOLOGICAL DIVERSITY

The Convention on Biological Diversity was signed by over 150 governments at the Rio "Earth Summit" in 1992 and entered into force in 1993. It has become the centerpiece of international efforts to conserve the planet's biological diversity, ensure the sustainable use of biological resources, protect ecosystems and natural habitats, and promote the fair and equitable sharing of the benefits arising from the utilization of genetic resources. The Convention was signed on June 4, 1993, but the U.S. has failed to ratify it.

KYOTO PROTOCOL TO THE UNITED NATIONS CONVENTION ON CLIMATE CHANGE

The agreement sets legally binding limits on the heat-trapping greenhouse gases that cause global warming. Under the protocol, industrialized countries agreed to reduce their overall emissions to about 5 percent below 1990 levels by 2012, with a range of specific reduction requirements for other countries. The United States signed the Protocol on November 12, 1998. In March 2001, President Bush withdrew from further negotiations and announced his intent to "unsign" the protocol.

OTHER MAJOR INTERNATIONAL TREATIES

INTERNATIONAL CRIMINAL COURT (ICC)

On July 17, 1998, 120 nations voted to establish the International Criminal Court (seven voted against the court including China, Israel, Iraq, and the United States) and 21 abstained. The International Criminal Court (ICC) will be able to investigate and prosecute those individuals accused of crimes against humanity, genocide, and crimes of war. The ICC will complement existing national judicial systems and step in only if national courts are unwilling or unable to investigate or prosecute such crimes. The ICC will also help defend the rights of those, such as women and children, who have often had little recourse to justice. The tribunal came into force on July 1, 2002. The Bush Administration has rejected the International Criminal Court and examined ways to withdraw the U.S. signature from the document creating the ICC. After the U.S. lost an appeal at the court to receive permanent immunity from prosecution it has attempted to secure immunity on a bilateral basis with signatories.

UN CONVENTION ON THE ELIMINATION OF ALL FORMS OF DISCRIMINATION AGAINST WOMEN (CEDAW)

CEDAW is an "international bill of rights for women" that has been ratified by every industrialized nation in the world except the United States. The treaty contains 30 articles including the establishment of an international tribunal to monitor violence, poverty, discrimination, lack of legal status, property rights, health care, education, and credit for women. CEDAW was signed by President Carter in 1980 but it has not been ratified by the Senate.

INTERNATIONAL LABOR ORGANIZATION (ILO)

The ILO, established by the Treaty of Versailles in 1919, is the UN agency dedicated to protecting labor standards, improving working condition, and promoting harmonious industrial relations. Conventions guarantee core labor rights to organize and engage in collective bargaining. While the United States is a member of the ILO it has failed to ratify 6 of the 8 major conventions, including those related to freedom of association, equality, the forced labor convention and the minimum age convention. Only two other states, Lao People's Democratic Republic and the Solomon Islands have ratified fewer conventions than the United States.

Sources: Department of State, *Major International Environment Agreements*, 1998. Available online at: http://www.state.gov/www/global/oes/envir_agreements.html. See also, Susan R. Fletcher, "International Environment: Current Major Global Treaties," Congressional Research Report, November 5, 1996.

Resources

WEB SITES

Afgha (Afghan news service)
www.afgha.com
Fax: +32-2-6125761

Alternet.org
www.alternet.org

AntiWar.com
www.antiwar.com

Asia Times online
www.Atimes.com

Counterpunch
www.counterpunch.org

Derechos Human Rights (Internet-based human rights)
www.derechos.org

Electronic Intifada
MECCS/EI Project
1507 E. 53rd Street, #500
Chicago, IL 60615
www.electronicintifada.net

Human Rights Internet
8 York Street, #302
Ottowa, Ontario K1N556
CANADA
www.hri.ca

Indymedia Center
www.indymedia.org/peace

MOVEON
www.moveon.org

NOW: The Truth About George
www.thetruthaboutgeorge.com

Oneworld.net
www.oneworld.net

RAWA
www.rawa.org
e-mail: Rawa@rawa.org

Salon.com
22 4th Street, 16th Floor
San Francisco, CA 94103
(415) 645-9200
www.salon.com

Terrorism Answers: CFR
Council on Foreign Relations
1779 Massachusetts Avenue NW
Washington, DC 20036
www.terrorismanswers.com
www.cfr.org

Z-Net
Foreign Policy Watch
www.zmag.org
www.zmag.org/ForPol/blumtop.htm

ORGANIZATIONS

50 Years Is Enough Network
3628 12th Street NE,
Washington, DC 20017 (202) 463-2265
www.50years.org

Africa Action
110 Maryland Avenue NE, #508
Washington, DC 20002
www.africaaction.org

American Arab Anti-Discrimination Committee
4201 Connecticut Avenue NW, Suite 300
Washington, DC 20002
(202) 244-2990
www.adc.org

Americans for Democratic Action
1625 K Street NW, #210
Washington, DC 20006
www.adaction.org

American Friends Service Committee
1501 Cherry Street
Philadelphia, PA 19102
(215) 241-7000
www.afsc.org

American Kurdish Information Network
2600 Connecticut Avenue, #1
Washington, DC 20008
(202) 483-6444
www.kurdistan.org

AMIDEAST
1730 M Street NW, Suite 1100
Washington, DC 20036-2882
(202) 785-1141
www.amideast.org

Amnesty International—USA
National Office
322 Eighth Avenue
New York, NY 10001
(212) 807-8400
www.aiusa.org

Arab American Institute
1600 K Street NW, Suite 601
Washington DC, 20006
(202) 429-9210
www.aaiusa.org

Arms Control Association
1726 M Street NW
Washington, DC 20036
(202) 463-8270
www.armscontrol.org/

Arms Trade Resource Center
World Policy Institute
66 Fifth Avenue, Suite 901
New York, NY 10011
(212) 229-5808
www.worldpolicy.org/projects/arms

Better World Campaign
1301 Connecticut Avenue NW, 5th Floor
Washington, DC 20036
(202) 462-4900
www.betterworldfund.org

CAIR
453 New Jersey Avenue SE
Washington, DC 20003-4034
(202) 488-8787
www.cair-net.org

Campaign for UN Reform
402 7th Street SE, Suite C
Washington, DC 20003
(888) 869-CUNR
www.cunr.org

Carnegie Endowment for International Peace
Foreign Policy magazine
1779 Massachusetts Avenue NW
Washington, DC 20036
(202) 483-7600
www.ceip.org

Center for Constitutional Rights
666 Broadway, 7th Floor
New York, NY 10012
(212) 614-6464
www.ccr-ny.org

Center for Contemporary Arab Studies
Georgetown University—ICC 241
Washington, DC 20057-1020
(202) 687-5793
www.ccasonline.org

Center for Defense Information
1779 Massachusetts Avenue NW
Washington, DC 20036
(202) 332-0600
www.cdi.org

Center for the Global South
American University
4400 Massachusetts Avenue NW
Washington, DC 20016
(202) 885-1619
www.amcrican.edu/academic.depts/acainst/cgs/index.html

Center for Policy Alternatives
1875 Connecticut Avenue NW, #710
Washington, DC 20009
(202) 387-6030
www.stateaction.org

Center for Public Integrity
910 17th Street NW, 7th Floor
Washington, DC 20006
(202) 466-1300
www.publicintegrity.org

Corpwatch
PO Box 29344
San Francisco, CA 94129
(415) 561-6568
www.corpwatch.org

Council for a Livable World
110 Maryland Avenue NE
Washington, DC 20002
www.clw.org

Drug Policy Alliance (Lindesmith Center)
925 15th Street NW, 2nd Floor
Washington, DC 20005
(202) 216-0035
www.drugpolicy.org

EPIC: Education for Peace in Iraq Center
1101 Pennsylvania Avenue SE
Washington, DC 20003
(202) 543-6176
www.epic-usa.org

Eurasia Foundation
1350 Connecticut Avenue NW, #1000
Washington, DC 20036
(202) 234-7370
www.eurasia.org

Federation of American Scientists
1717 K Street NW, Suite 209
Washington, DC 20036
(202) 546-3300
www.fas.org

Foreign Policy in Focus
Institute for Policy Studies
733 15th Street NW, Suite 1020
Washington, DC 20005
(202) 234-9382
www.fpif.org

Foreign Policy in Focus
Interhemispheric Resource Center
Box 2178
Silver City, NM 88062
(505) 388-0208
www.fpif.org

Fourth Freedom Forum
11 Dupont Circle, Ninth Floor
Washington, DC 20036
(202) 393-5201
www.fourthfreedom.org

Friends Committee on National Legislation
245 2nd Street NE
Washington, DC 20002
(202) 547-6000
www.fcnl.org

Global Exchange
2017 Mission Street, #303
San Francisco, CA 94110
(415) 255-7296
www.globalexchange.org

Global Policy Forum
777 UN Plaza, Suite 7G
New York, NY 10017
(212) 557-3161
www.globalpolicy.org

Human Rights Watch
350 Fifth Avenue, 34th Floor
New York, NY 10118
www.hrw.org

Institute for Defense and Disarmament Studies
675 Massachusetts Avenue
Cambridge, MA 02139
(617) 354-IDDS (4337)
www.idds.org

International Center for Research on Women
1717 Massachusetts Avenue NW, #302
Washington, DC 20036
(202) 797-0007
www.icrw.org

Latin America Working Group
110 Maryland Avenue NE
Box 15
Washington, DC 20002
(202) 797-2171
www.lawg.org

Lawyers Committee for Human Rights
100 Maryland Avenue NW, #500
Washington, DC 20002
(202) 547-5692
333 7th Avenue, 13th Floor
New York, NY 10001
www.lchr.org

MERIP
1500 Massachusetts Avenue NW, Suite 119
Washington, DC 20005
(202) 223-3677
www.merip.org

National Security Archive
George Washington University
2130 H Street NW, #701
Washington, DC 20037
(202) 994-7000
www.gwu.edu/~nsarchiv/

Policy Action Network (EPN)
Moving Ideas Network
2000 L Street NW, #717
Washington, DC 20036
(202) 776-0730
www.movingideas.org

Project on Defense Alternatives
Commonwealth Institute
PO Box 348105
Inman Square Post Office
Cambridge, MA 02139
www.comw.org/pda

Project on Government Oversight
666 11th Street NW, #500
(202) 347-1122
www.pogo.org

SOA Watch
PO Box 4566
Washington, DC 20017
(202) 234-3440
www.soaw.org

UN Association—USA
801 Second Avenue, 2nd Floor
New York, NY 10017
(212) 907-1300
www.unausa.org

UN Foundation
1301 Connecticut Avenue NW, #700
Washington, DC 20036
(202) 887-9040
www.unfoundation.org

U.S. Committee for Refugees/IRSA
1717 Massachusetts Avenue NW, #200
Washington, DC 20036
www.refugees.org
www.refugeesusa.org

Washington Office on Latin America
1630 Connecticut Avenue NW, Suite 200
Washington, DC 2009
(202) 797-2171
www.wola.org

Women in International Security (WIIS)
Center for Peace and Security Studies,
Edmund A. Walsh School of Foreign Service, Georgetown University
Box 571145, Washington, DC 20005
(202) 687-3366
www.wiis.org

Women's Action for New Directions (WAND)
110 Maryland Avenue NE, #205
Washington, DC 20002
(202) 543-8505
www.wand.org

Women's International League for Peace and Freedom (WILPF)
1213 Race Street
Philadelphia, PA 19107
(215) 563-7110
www.wilpf.org

World Federalist Association
418 Seventh Street SE
Washington, DC 20003
(202) 546-3950
www.wfa.org

WorldWatch Institute
1776 Massachusetts Avenue NW
Washington, DC 20036
(202) 452-1999
www.worldwatch.org

RESOURCES/OUTLETS

American Prospect
2000 L Street NW, Suite 717
Washington, DC 20036
1-888-MUST-READ
www.prospect.org

Bill Moyers NOW: PBS
www.pbs.org/now/

Bulletin of Atomic Scientists
6042 South Kimbark Avenue
Chicago, IL 60637
(773) 702-2555
www.thebulletin.org

C-SPAN
www.c-span.org/terrorism

Far Eastern Economic Review
Review Publishing Company Limited
GPO Box 160
Hong Kong
www.feer.com

Frontline Documentaries: PBS
www.pbs.org/frontline

Harvard Project on Cold War Studies
www.fas.harvard.edu/~hpcws/

Independent Television Services (ITVS)
www.itvs.org

Inter Press Service
www.ips.org
National Public Radio
635 Massachusetts Avenue NW
Washington, DC 20001
(202) 513-2000
www.npr.org

News Hour: PBS
www.pbs.org.newshour/

Peace and World Security Studies
School of Social Science
Hampshire College
Amherst, MA 01002
(413) 559-5367
www.pawss.hampshire.edu

The Progressive
409 East Main Street
Madison, WI 53703
(608) 257-4626
www.progressive.org

INTERNATIONAL ORGANIZATIONS

European Union
www.eurunion.org

International Committee of the Red Cross
19 Avenue de la Pais
CH 1202 Geneve, SUISSE
+41-22-734-6001
www.icrc.org

International Security Information Service (ISIS)—Europe
Rue Archimède 5, B-1000
Brussels, Belgium
+32-2-230 7446
www.isis-europe.org

Islamonline.net
Doha-Qatar
P.O. Box 22212
+974-447-0444
www.islamonline.net
Stockholm International Peace Research Institute
www.sipri.se
www.sipri.org

Stopthewar.org.uk
P.O. Box 3739
London E5 & EJ
+44 (0) -7951-235-915
www.stopthewar.org.uk

United Nations
www.un.org

U.S. GOVERNMENT

Department of Defense
www.defenselink.mil

House Committee on International Relations www.house.gov/international_relations/

Senate Foreign Relations Committee
www.foreign.senate.gov

State Department
www.state.gov

Notes

INTRODUCTION

1 Immanuel Wallerstein, "The Eagle Has Crash Landed," *Foreign Policy*, Summer 2002. Wallerstein cites Bush's handling of the downed U.S. plane in China in April 2001 as a prime example.

2 Colum Lynch, "Al Qaeda Is Reviving, U.N. Report Says," *Washington Post*, 18 December 2002.

3 Carl Conetta, *Strange Victory*, Research Monograph #6 (Boston: Project on Defense Alternatives, January 2002), available at www.comw.org/pda/0201strangevic.html.

4 Ibid.

5 "The National Security Strategy of the United States of America" is a summary that administrations have presented to Congress every year since 1986. The Bush administration submitted its most recent summary in September 2002. See David Sanger, "Changes in Strategy," *New York Times*, September 20, 2002.

6 See, e.g., Charles Clover, "Dreams of the Eurasian Heartland: The Reemergence of Geopolitics," *Foreign Affairs*, March/April 1999.

7 Zbigniew Brzezinski explicitly revived the Eurasian strategy in *The Grand Chessboard* (New York: Basic Books, 1997).

8 For a partial list of U.S. unilateralism at the UN in the 1980s, see William Blum, *Rogue State* (Monroe, ME: Common Courage Press, 2000), 185-97.

9 Walter Russell Mead, *Special Providence: American Foreign Policy and How It Changed the World* (New York: Knopf, 2001), 290.

10 William Shawcross, *Deliver Us from Evil* (New York: Simon and Schuster, 2000), 123.

11 Wayne Smith, "The Trend Toward Unilateralism in U.S. Foreign Policy," Center for International Policy, November 1999.

12 Charles William Maynes, "America's Fading Commitment to the World," in Martha Honey and Tom Barry, eds., *Global Focus* (New York: St. Martin's Press, 2000), 93.

13 The distinction between Clinton objectives and Congressional politicking was lost on foreign observers who, based on their own systems, expected chief executives to have primary control over foreign policy. What might then appear domestically as a pitched battle between a president upholding multilateral norms and a Congress committed to preserving U.S. sovereignty registered

abroad in the final analysis simply as a unilateralist administration that made duplicitous commitments to cooperative undertakings.

14 According to a study by Steven Holloway of U.S. voting behavior at the UN, the United States voted against the majority in 31.5 percent of all votes in 1976, 53.4 percent in 1981 (Reagan's first year), 60.5 percent in 1992 (Bush Sr.'s last year) and 57.6 percent in 1993 (Clinton's first year). The transition from Bush to Clinton did not restore the pre-Reagan commitment to multilateralism. The gap in voting between the United States and its NATO allies is even more telling, increasing dramatically during this period from 13 points in 1980 to 36 points in 1992 and 30 points in 1993. Standing outside the majority, the United States was increasingly left without even the comfort of its allies. Steven Holloway, "U.S. Unilateralism at the UN: Why Great Powers Do Not Make Great Multilateralists," *Global Governance*, July 2000.

15 Joseph Nye, *The Paradox of American Power* (New York: Oxford University Press, 2002), 16.

16 As one analyst notes, "The U.S. practiced free trade in areas of its comparative advantage, while being protectionist in other areas; and it gave trade concessions to countries that were important to its security interests, while holding others to free trade." Anthony Tuo-Kofi Gadzey, *The Political Economy of Power: Hegemony and Economic Liberalism* (Houndsmill, England: Macmillan, 1994), 104–10.

17 Warren Christopher in his first appearance before the Senate Foreign Relations Committee. Quoted in Michael Klare, *Resource Wars* (New York: Metropolitan Books, 2001), 8.

18 For more background, see Stewart Patrick, "Don't Fence Me In: The Perils of Going It Alone," *World Policy Journal*, Fall 2001.

CHAPTER ONE: HOW THINGS HAVE CHANGED

19 Jim Lobe, "Army Peacekeeping Institute Sent Packing," TomPaine.com, 17 July 2002.

20 George W. Bush, "A Period of Consequences," Speech delivered at the Citadel, 23 September 1999, available at citadel.edu/pao/addresses/pres_bush.html.

21 *Wall Street Journal*, 19 July 2002.

22 Ian Williams, "The U.S. Hit List at the United Nations," (Silver City, NM & Washington, DC: Foreign Policy in Focus, 30 April 2002).

23 For an excellent treatment of ways realism and liberal internationalism combined to shape the U.S. grand strategy during the Cold War see: G. John Ikenberry, "America's Imperial Ambition," *Foreign Affairs*, September/October 2002.

24 An early argument to this effect came from neo-conservative godfather Irving Kristol at the American Enterprise Institute. Kristol, "The Emerging American Imperium," August 1997, available at www.aei.org/oti/otii7998.htm.

25   John Bolton, undersecretary of state for arms control, is the most outspoken opponent of multilateralism within the administration, representing the right wing's ideological opposition to global governance. However, it has been National Security Adviser Condoleezza Rice who has best articulated the administration's pragmatic posture with respect to multilateralism. During the campaign, she criticized the Democrats for subordinating U.S. national interests to "the interests of an illusory international community" and for maintaining the liberal "belief that the support of many states—or even better, of institutions like the United Nations—is essential to the legitimate exercise of power." While not completely rejecting all instances of multilateralism, the administration would pick and choose—what the State Department's director of policy planning called "multilateralism a la carte." It has long been accepted that nations must act unilaterally to defend their most basic interests—a practice described by the Clinton administration as "multilateral when we can, unilateral when we must." The Bush administration, in contrast, rejects the post–World War II premise that multilateralism is generally the best route in the pursuit of national interests. For an exploration of these themes, see Stewart Patrick, "Don't Fence Me In."

26   Ikenberry, *Foreign Affairs*, September/October 2002. The growing size of the multilateral web is not the paranoiac perception of rightist ideologues but a fact of international relations. "Between 1970 and 1997, the number of international treaties more than tripled, and from 1985–1999 alone, the number of international institutions increased by two-thirds." Stewart Patrick, "Multilateralism and Its Discontents: Causes and Consequences of U.S. Ambivalence," in Patrick and Shephard Forman, eds., *Multilateralism and U.S. Foreign Policy* (Boulder, Colo.: Lynne Rienner Publishers, 2002), 12.

27   The first analyst to liken the Bush administration's philosophy of power to that of Hobbes was Jim Lobe. See Jim Lobe, "Welcome to a Hobbesian World," Inter Press Service, March 9, 2001.

28   In the U.S. international affairs budget, 93 percent is dedicated to the military and 7 percent to the State Department.

29   Dana Priest, "A Four-Star Foreign Policy? U.S. Commanders Wield Rising Clout," *Washington Post*, 28 September 2000, A1; "Reinventing War," *Foreign Policy*, November/December 2001, 127: 31–47.

30   "Q & A with Donald Rumsfeld," *Chicago Sun-Times*, 18 November 2001.

31   Michael Klare, "Endless Military Superiority," *The Nation*, 15 July 2002.

32   Russell E. Travers, "The New Millennium and a Strategic Breathing Space," *The Washington Quarterly*, Spring 1997.

33   Richard Falk, "The New Bush Doctrine," *The Nation*, 15 July 2002.

34   In a precautionary addendum, one that may speak to U.S. supremacist hubris, John Winthrop warned that should we fail to make our city on the hill a model of hope and virtue and should we "deal falsely with our God," then we would be cursed. James Chace, "Imperial America and the Common Interest," *World Policy Journal*, Winter 2002.

35   For a representative presentation of this argument, see Robert Kagan, *Policy Review*, June/July 2002, available at www.ceip.org/files/print/2002-06-02-policyreview.htm. Kagan's lead sentence advises, "It is time to stop pretending that Europeans and Americans share a common view of the world, or even that they occupy the same world."

CHAPTER TWO: THE PEOPLE

36   Barton Gellman, "Keeping the U.S. First; Pentagon Would Preclude a Rival Superpower," *Washington Post*, 11 March 1992, 1.

37   Todd S. Purdum, "Embattled, Scrutinized, Powell Soldiers On," *New York Times*, 25 July 2002.

38   The National Security Strategy document not only mirrored the Defense Policy Guideline of 1992 but also the security strategy document produced in September 2001 by the Project for the New American Century, entitled *Rebuilding America's Defenses: Strategy, Forces, and Resources for the New Century.*

39   A blueprint for the new radical foreign policy is found in a book published during the presidential campaign and edited by PNAC founders that includes chapters by men who are now part of the Bush foreign policy team, including Peter Rodman, Elliott Abrams, Richard Perle, and Paul Wolfowitz, as well as other leading neoconservatives such as William Bennett, Donald Kagan, and Reuel Marc Gerecht. See Robert Kagan and William Kristol, eds., *Present Dangers: Crisis and Opportunity in American Foreign and Defense Policy* (San Francisco: Encounter Books, 2000).

40   Charles Krauthammer, "The Unipolar Moment," *Foreign Affairs*, vol. 70, no. 1 (Winter 1990–91).

41   Key parts of the right-wing anticommunist coalition—particularly the libertarians and "paleo-conservatives" such as Pat Buchanan—strongly opposed the imperial vision of the kind that Krauthammer and fellow neoconservatives were proposing.

42   Tom Barry and Jim Lobe, "Foreign Policy: Right Face, Forward March," (Silver City, NM & Washington, DC: Foreign Policy in Focus, April 2002).

43   Statement of Principles, Project for the New American Century, 3 June 1997, www.newamericancentury.org/statementofprinciples.htm.

44   PNAC boosters have not shied away from the notion of an imperium. See, for example, Dan Balz quoting William Kristol in "In War Reversal, Criticism is Mostly From Right," *Washington Post*, 26 November 2001.

45   In addition to Robert Kagan and William Kristol, other neo-conservatives that have associated themselves with PNAC include Elliott Abrams, Eliot Cohen, Midge Decter, Francis Fukuyama, Jeane Kirkpatrick, Norman Podheretz, and George Weigel. Prominent social conservatives associated with PNAC include Gary Bauer, William Bennett, Steve Forbes, Dan Quayle, and Vin Weber. Hawks or national security militarists include Richard Cheney, Frank Gafney, Zalmay Khalilzad, I. Lewis Libby, Richard Perle, Peter Rodman, Donald Rumsfeld, Paul Wolfowitz, and R. James Woolsey.

46 Sara Diamond, *Roads to Dominion: Right-Wing Movements and Political Power in the United States* (New York: Guilford Press, 1996), 178–202.

47 See Diamond, *Roads to Dominion*, for excellent treatment of fusionist trends in the right until the mid-1990s. According to Diamond, the New Right of the 1970s and 1980s "represented a reassertion of the old fusionist blend of anti-communism, traditionalism, and libertarianism," but with more emphasis on moral traditionalism than given by the fusionists of the 1950s.

48 Daniel Patrick Moynihan, *Pandaemonium: Ethnicity in International Politics* (New York: Oxford University Press, 1993), 36: "They wished for a military posture approaching mobilization; they would create or invent whatever crises were required to bring this about."

49 For the influence of the Center for National Security and arms manufacturers, see William Hartung, *Military Industrial Complex Revisited*, (Silver City, NM & Washington, DC: Foreign Policy in Focus, June 1999), available at www.fpif.org/papers/micr/index.html. See also Jason Vest, "The Men from JINSA and CSP," *The Nation*, 2–9 September 2002.

50 Ethics and Public Policy Center, "About EPPC," available at www.eppc.org/about/xq/ASP/qx/about.htm.

51 Samuel P. Huntington, *The Clash of Civilizations and the Remaking of World Order* (New York: Simon & Schuster, 1996).

52 See also William Bennett, *Why We Fight: Moral Clarity and the War on Terrorism* (New York: Doubleday, 2002).

53 *New York Times*, 10 March 2002.

54 Nicholas Kristof, "The New Internationalists," *New York Times*, 21 May 2002.

55 For a helpful examination of the links between the Christian Right and the largely Jewish neoconservatives, see Chip Berlet and Matthew N. Lyons, *Right-Wing Populism in America: Too Close for Comfort* (New York: Guilford Press, 2000). The founders of neoconservative thought, Irving Kristol, Midge Decter, and Gertrude Himmelfarb, defend the Christian Right, declaring that on "the survival of Israel, the Jews have no more stalwart friends than evangelical Christians," if for no other reason than the millennialist and dispensationalist beliefs of the Christian Right revolve around an apocalyptic showdown in Jerusalem (Berlet and Lyons, 263). See also Sara Diamond, *Roads to Dominion*.

56 The three principals of the Foundation for Defense of Democracies, founded in the wake of 9/11, are Jack Kemp, Jeane Kirkpatrick, and Steve Forbes.

57 Negroponte, Bush's UN ambassador, served as ambassador to Honduras during the height of the contra war and the Honduran government's internal campaign of repression against leftists and human rights advocates. As assistant secretary of state for Latin America under President Reagan, Abrams oversaw the administration's covert campaign to aid the contras. He pleaded guilty to two charges of withholding information from Congress. Poindexter, who was hired by the Pentagon to head its Information Awareness Office, was Reagan's national security adviser and was the point man in the Iran-contra scandal. Reich's

Office of Public Diplomacy for Latin America and the Caribbean was closed as the result of congressional inquiries into the covert funding of the contras.

58 For more on the connections between AEI and the Bush administration, see Jim Lobe, "The Axis of Incitement," Inter Press Service, 6 March 2002.

59 Working with Perle at AEI, in addition to Lynne Cheney, are several other neo-conservatives who have played important roles in expanding the list of potential targets for the administration's war on terrorism, including Michael Ledeen, who cofounded JINSA with Gaffney; former CIA officer Reuel Marc Gerecht, who also heads PNAC's Mideast project; and Michael Rubin, who was hired by the Pentagon to help prepare the groundwork for a post-Hussein Iraq. Ledeen, who gained notoriety as an intermediary between Oliver North and the Iranians in the Iran-contra affairs, and Gerecht have both been especially outspoken about promoting a pro-U.S. uprising in Iran.

60 Jim Lobe and Tom Barry, "U.S. Middle East Policy: 'Enough is Enough,'" (Silver City, NM & Washington, DC: Foreign Policy in Focus, April 2002), available at www.fpif.org/commentary/2002/0204pnac.html.

61 This pragmatic application of free trade philosophy to U.S. foreign economic policy is the prevailing approach of conservatives (and most liberal policy makers, as well) in pursuing economic supremacy. However, within this general framework, there are bitter divisions. The nationalist and reactionary populist right wing, as epitomized by Pat Buchanan, contends that Washington increasingly measures U.S. economic interests by what is good for footloose U.S. corporations rather than the American people and domestic production. The populist Right is more apt to support protectionist measures than the dominant internationalists of the Republican Party, who respond primarily to the interests of corporate donors. A similar split within the right regarding international economic policy revolves around U.S. sanctions. Unilateral economic sanctions are generally opposed by the right's Wall Street donors but are heartily supported by right-wing populists and neoconservatives. A powerful coalition of business interests complains that the imposition of economic sanctions in response to violations of human rights and other international norms has the effect of handicapping U.S. corporations and undermining the drive for U.S. economic supremacy. This business-first approach infuriates the moral, political, and military ideologues of the right, who believe that the United States should severely restrict or condition its business dealings with respect to such considerations as national security, anticommunism, and the repression of religious minorities, principally Christians. For more on the divisions within the right on economic supremacy concerns, see Tom Barry and Jim Lobe, "U.S. Foreign Policy—Attention, Right Face, Forward March."

62 This objective of military supremacy was expressed by General Colin Powell in 1992 when he declared that the United States needed the military might "to deter any challenger from ever dreaming of challenging us on the world stage." The difference, however, is that the neoconservatives believe that U.S. supremacy requires America to act preemptively to prevent the emergence of threats to U.S. power—a doctrine that makes the realists and moderate conservatives

nervous, although they too have signed on to what is now official U.S. security doctrine. See Anatol Lieven, "The Push for War," *London Review of Books,* 3 October 2002.

CHAPTER THREE: THE POLICIES

RESOURCES

63 National Energy Policy Development Group (Washington, D.C., May 2001), x; ch. 8: 3.

64 U.S. Department of Energy, Energy Information Administration, *International Energy Outlook 2002* (Washington, D.C., 2002), 183, 242.

65 *National Energy Policy,* ch. 8: 4.

66 U.S. Department of Defense (DoD), *Quadrennial Defense Review Report* (Washington, D.C.: DoD, 30 September 2001), 4.

67 American military strategy "rests on the assumption that U.S. forces have the ability to project power worldwide," the QDR declares. "The United States must retain the capability to send well-armed and logistically supported forces to critical points around the globe, even in the face of enemy opposition...." Ibid., 43.

68 George W. Bush, "A Period of Consequences," Speech delivered at the Citadel, 23 September 1999, available at citadel.edu/pao/addresses/pres_bush.html.

69 Remarks of Donald Rumsfeld at the National Defense University, Washington, D.C., 31 January 31 2002, available at www.defenselink.mil/cgi-bin/dlprint.cgi (posted 9 March 2002).

70 The author first advanced this argument in "The Geopolitics of War," *The Nation,* 5 November 2001, 11–15. For a similar analysis, see "Line in the Sand: Saudi Role in Alliance Fuels Religious Tension in Oil-Rich Kingdom," *Wall Street Journal,* 4 October 2001.

71 For background on these efforts, see Michael T. Klare, *Resource Wars: The New Landscape of Global Conflict* (New York: Metropolitan Books / Henry Holt, 2001), 1–5, 81–108.

72 U.S. Department of State, *Congressional Budget Justification: Foreign Operations, Fiscal Year 2003* (Washington, D.C., 2002), 309.

73 See the justifications provided by the Department of State for increased levels of U.S. assistance to these countries in ibid., 287–341.

MILITARY

74 By contrast, Ronald Reagan came into office spouting similar unilateralist rhetoric, but his administration evolved under public pressure to the point that it not only did not abandon the Anti-Ballistic Missile Treaty but actually negotiated and signed important new arms accords such as the Intermediate Nuclear Forces in Europe Treaty (INF) and the Strategic Arms Reduction Treaty (START). And while Bush policy makers seek to unleash the full spectrum of

interventionary options, including U.S. ground troops, Reagan's preferred form of intervention was via covert arms sales to anticommunist rebel groups from Angola to Afghanistan.

75 For details on Bush's defense policy views during the campaign, see George W. Bush, "A Period of Consequences," Speech delivered at the Citadel, 23 September 1999, available at citadel.edu/pao/addresses/pres_bush.html.

76 For a synopsis of Bush's and Gore's respective positions on military spending on the campaign trail, see "From Social Security to Environment, the Candidates' Positions," *New York Times*, 5 November 2000.

77 The Bush administration inherited an FY 2001 budget for national defense (including the Pentagon and nuclear weapons spending at the Department of Energy) of $309 billion, which was increased to $343 billion in FY 2002 and $393 billion in FY 2003 (final levels to be determined pending results of a House-Senate conference in fall 2002). In addition, two supplemental appropriations for the Pentagon have been approved, one for $18 billion in September 2001 and the other for $15 billion in July 2002, for a total of $151 billion in new military spending approved since the Bush administration took office. For details on the military budget, see the Web sites of the Center for Strategic and Budgetary Assessments, www.csbaonline.org, and the Center for Defense Information, www.cdi.org, and the Pentagon comptroller's budget information site, www.dtic.mil/comptroller/fy2003budget/.

78 Analysis by the author, utilizing Pentagon budget documents including *Program Acquisition Costs by Weapons System* for FY 2002 and FY 2003, plus the P-1 and R-1 detailed breakdowns on procurement and R&D spending, all available at For estimates of the cost of the war in Afghanistan, see Steven Kosiak, *Estimates of the Cost of Operation Enduring Freedom: The First Two Months*, Center on Strategic and Budgetary Assessments, 7 December 2001. On the issue of missile defense and terrorism, top U.S. intelligence analysts have repeatedly pointed out that a long-range ballistic missile is the least likely method a nation-state adversary, much less a terrorist group, would use to deliver a weapon of mass destruction against a target in the United States, because it would be a simple matter to identify the nation of origin and subject it to a devastating retaliatory strike. If a terrorist group were to get hold of a chemical, biological, or nuclear weapon, it would be far more likely to try to bring it into the United States in a shipping container or a truck than via a three-stage, multiton ballistic missile.

79 George C. Wilson, "Is Crusader the Beginning, or the End of Reform?" *National Journal*, 11 May 2001.

80 On total contracts, see U.S. Department of Defense, *100 Companies Receiving the Largest Amount of Prime Contract Awards from the Department of Defense, FY 2001*; on companies benefiting from Coast Guard and other U.S. government contracts, see company Web sites at www.lockheed.com, www.northropgrumman.com, www.boeing.com, and www.raytheon.com.

81 U.S. Department of Defense, *Quadrennial Defense Review Report* (hereafter referred to as *QDR Report*), 30 September 2001, 2. A number of African nations might also be singled out for U.S. military intervention under the rubric of deal-

ing with "weak states" that harbor terrorists or criminal syndicates, which is discussed later in this section.

82   Ibid., 4.

83   Ibid., 18.

84   "In several regions, the inability of some states to govern their societies, safeguard their military armaments, and prevent their territories from serving as sanctuary to terrorists and criminal organizations can also pose a threat to stability and place demands on U.S. forces," *QDR Report*, 5.

85   Ibid., 17–18.

86   "The National Security Strategy of the United States of America," September 2002, 1, available at http://www.whitehouse.gov/nsc/nss.html.

87   Quotations in this paragraph are from "The National Security Strategy of the United States," 6, 14.

88   William M. Arkin, "The Best Defense: A Classified Planning Document Describes Bold New Weapons and Preemptive Strategic Offenses. But Will It Lead to the Kind of World We Want To Live In?" *Los Angeles Times*, 14 July 2002.

89   William M. Arkin, "Secret Plan Outlines the Unthinkable," *Los Angeles Times*, 10 March 2002.

90   The administration is already seeking funding to accelerate the development of low-yield nuclear weapons, while the notion of nuclear-armed missile interceptors is being considered by the Defense Science Board, an influential Pentagon advisory panel. See Arkin, "Secret Plan"; and Bradley Graham, "Going Backwards: Nuclear-Tipped Interceptors Studied," *Washington Post*, 12 March 2002.

91   United States Space Command, "Vision for 2020" (Washington, D.C: U.S. Space Command, February 1997), 1–3.

92   Ibid., 4.

93   See Robert Wall, "Rumsfeld Revamps Space, Pushes 'Black' Projects," *Aviation Week and Space Technology*, 14 May 2001. Before joining the Bush administration, Rumsfeld chaired the Commission to Assess the United States National Security Space Management and Organization, which stated "It is...possible to project power through and from space in response to events anywhere in the world. Having this capability would give the United States a much stronger deterrent, and, in a conflict, an extraordinary military advantage." The quote from the commission is cited in Theresa Hitchens, "Space Weapons: More Security or Less?" in James Clay Moltz, ed., *Future Security in Space: Commercial, Military, and Arms Control Trade-Offs*, a joint publication of the Monterrey Institute for International Studies and the Mountbatten Centre for International Studies (University of Southampton, 2002), 28.

94   At a March 6, 2001, conference in Washington, former Lockheed Martin chief operating officer and current Undersecretary of the Air Force Peter B. Teets, who is in charge of coordinating the acquisition of military space assets, said, "I believe that weapons will go into space. It's a question of time. And we need to

be at the forefront of that." Theresa Hitchens, "Weapons In Space: Silver Bullet or Russian Roulette?" Center for Defense Information, 18 April 2002, 2.

95   "Faking Restraint: The Bush Administration's Secret Plan for Strengthening U.S. Nuclear Forces," (Washington, D.C: Natural Resources Defense Council, 13 February 2002); and William D. Hartung, "Making the World Safe For Nuclear Weapons," *Alternet*, 15 May 2002.

96   On U.S. arms and aid policies under the Bush administration, see Tamar Gabelnick, "Security Assistance After September 11," (Silver City, NM & Washington, DC: Foreign Policy in Focus, May 2002); and Michelle Ciarrocca, "American Arms—Into Whose Hands?", Motherjones.com, 21 February 21 2002.

97   Frida Berrigan, "Actions Speak Against Words: President Bush is Deepening U.S. Ties with Countries That Commit Human Rights Abuses," *Baltimore Sun*, 7 April 2002.

98   Ahmed Rashid, "Realpolitik Intrudes on Afghan Army: Western Allies Say U.S. Loath to Offend Warlords, Hesitates to Build Force," *Wall Street Journal*, 29 July 2002. The article notes that not only has the U.S. been reluctant to disarm the forces of regional warlords, who far outnumber the proposed Afghan national army, but that "[a]ides to President Karzai say that even as the Bush administration seeks to build a new military, the U.S. is still funding warlord armies in the southern and eastern provinces" of Afghanistan.

99   Under the 1994 agreement, North Korea agreed to curb its nuclear and ballistic missile programs in exchange for a U.S. pledge of nonaggression and a specific series of steps to assist North Korea with food and energy resources. The Bush administration's hostile rhetoric toward Pyongyang and its unwillingness to carry out the other steps set forth in the agreement set the stage for North Korea's decision to restart its nuclear program in the winter of 2002–2003. For background on this point, see Leon V. Sigal, "North Korea Is No Iraq: Pyongyang's Negotiating Strategy," *Arms Control Today*, December 2002, 8–12. As of January 2003, diplomatic efforts to head off the crisis remain stalled in part due to the Bush administration's unwillingness to negotiate directly with Pyongyang.

100   "Reinventing War," *Foreign Policy*, November–December 2001.

INTERNATIONAL LAW

101   Agence France Presse, 13 March 2002.

102   "EU's Patten criticises US foreign policy," BBC News, February 9, 2002.

103   Mark Matthews, "Bush to Issue 'Strike First' Strategy: Doctrine of Attacking Enemies Pre-Emptively Marks Major Policy Shift," *Baltimore Sun*, 30 June 2002, 1.

104   Glenn Kessler, "Concerns Over War Crimes Court Not New," *Washington Post*, 2 July 2002.

105   Suzann Chapman, "U.S. Renounces World Court Treaty," *Air Force Magazine*, June 2002, 16.

106 Inter Press Service, 10 July 2002.

107 David Wastell, "UN Deal," *Sunday Daily Telegraph*, 14 July 2002.

108 *Convention Relative to the Treatment of Prisoners of War*, 12 August 1949, Article 5, 6 U.S.T. 3316, 75 UNT.S 135.

109 Darcy Christen, a spokesperson for the ICRC, said of the detainees: "They were captured in combat [and] we consider them prisoners of war."The United Nations High Commissioner for Human Rights also found that such hearings were required: "The legal status of the detainees and their entitlement to prisoner of war (POW) status, if disputed, must be determined by a competent tribunal, in accordance with the provisions of Article 5 of the Third Geneva Convention." *Statement of High Commissioner for Human Rights on Detention of Taliban and Al Qaida Prisoners at US Base in Guantanamo Bay, Cuba*, 16 January 2002, available at www. unhchr.ch/huricane/huricane.nsf/newsroom.

110 "OAS Tribunal Asks U.S. to Heed Geneva Conventions on Guantanamo Detainees," 13 March 2002, available at www.humanrightsnow.org/oasconventiononguantanamodetainees.htm.

111 Geoff Dyer, Stephen Fidler, and Alexander Nicoll, "The Weapons Threat," *Financial Times*, 10 July 2002, 9.

FOREIGN ECONOMIC POLICY

112 Quoted in Nicholas Kristof, "What Does and Does Not Fuel Terrorism," *International Herald Tribune*, 8 May 2002.

113 Quoted in William Neikirk's "Trade Measure Has Close Call, Clears House," *Chicago Tribune*, 7 December 2001, 16.

114 Michael Wines, "Yeltsin Agrees to Closer Ties with Belarus,"*New York Times*, 26 December 1998, Section A, 1.

115 In previous decades when there were stronger popular movements, e.g., in Latin America and Central America through the 1980s (and Haiti in the early 1990s), the United States resorted much more frequently to violence. It is also worth noting that even today, in such cases (e.g., Venezuela, where Washington supported an attempted coup in April) the target government is often one that can resist the cartel because it has oil.

116 See Weisbrot, Naiman, and Kim, "The Emperor has No Growth: Declining Economic Growth Rates in the Era of Globalization," Center for Economic and Policy Research, 26 September 2000, available at www.cepr.net/globalization/The_Emperor_Has_No_Growth.htm.

117 See Mark Weisbrot, "The Mirage of Progress," *American Prospect* 13(1), available at www.prospect.org/print/V13/1/weisbrot-m.html.

118 See Mark Weisbrot, "Globalization for Whom?" *Cornell International Law Journal* 31(3) (1998), available at www.cepr.net/Globalization.html.

119 In a transcript of an interview for Stanford's Hoover Institute–sponsored TV program *Uncommon Knowledge*, Taylor asserted that the IMF "should be abolished…in

a way that takes some of the talents there and use[s] it in a more effective way."
See www.uncommonknowledge.org/99winter/320.html.

120 For an economic analysis of the unsustainability of Brazil's debt, see Weisbrot and Baker, "Paying the Bills in Brazil: Does the IMF's Math Add Up?" (Washington, DC: Center for Economic and Policy Research, 2002).

121 Louis Uchitelle, "Calculated Risk: U.S. and I.M.F. Lead Push for Brazil Bailout Plan," *New York Times*, 28 September 1998, 1.

122 See Ciblis, Weisbrot, and Kar, "Argentina Since Default: The IMF and the Depression" (Center for Economic and Policy Research, 2002), available at cepr.net/argentina_since_default.htm.

123 George Soros, *George Soros on Globalization* (New York: PublicAffairs, 2002).

124 See Ciblis, Weisbrot, and Kar, "Argentina Since Default."

125 The economy has lost more than 20 percent of its output since the last business cycle peak in 1998.

126 See Weisbrot and Baker, "The Relative Impact of Trade Liberalization on Developing Countries" (Washington, DC: Center for Economic and Policy Research, 2002).

127 See Public Citizen, "Drug Industry: Prices, Profits, R&D, Campaign Contributions & Lobbying," available at www.citizen.org/congress/reform/drug_industry/.

128 From 1997 to 2000 the United States threatened South Africa with economic sanctions for its Medicines Act, which allowed for the import of cheaper anti-AIDS drugs; protests in the United States forced the administration to abandon these efforts. Similarly, in January 2001 the Clinton administration challenged—through the WTO—Brazil's laws dealing with the manufacture and import of generic AIDS drugs. These laws formed an important part of Brazil's remarkably successful AIDS treatment program, which has cut by half the number of AIDS-related deaths there in recent years. The Brazilian government stood firm, and Washington dropped its case the following June.

129 This is a drastic change from the first half of the post–World War II era, during which the real median wage increased by about 80 percent (1946–73).

130 See Weisbrot and Baker, "Relative Impact of Trade Liberalization."

131 "No Deal Yet in World Bank Grants Versus Loan Dispute," *Transition Newsletter*, available at www.worldbank.org/transitionnewsletter/marapr02/pgs26-27.htm.

132 This faction, led by House Majority leader Dick Armey, defeated an $18 billion (50 percent) quota increase for the IMF ($90 billion when matched by other member countries) on three votes in 1998. It eventually passed Congress because there was almost no opposition in the Senate. But the world would be a different place today if the House Republican leadership had prevailed, with low- and middle-income countries facing a considerably less powerful creditors' cartel and possibly having more choices with regard to economic policy.

133 Joseph Stiglitz, *Globalization and Its Discontents* (New York: Norton, 2002).

134 Paul Krugman, "The Lost Continent," *New York Times*, 9 August 2002.

INTELLIGENCE

135 Senator Bob Graham (D-FL) and Representative Porter Goss (R-FL) are the chairmen of the intelligence committees.

136 Joint Inquiry Staff, "Joint Inquiry Staff Statement: Part I," 18 September 2002, available at www.fas.org/irp/congress/2002_hr/091802hill.html.

137 *New York Times*, 23 September 2002, 1.

138 *Wall Street Journal*, 13 May 1998, 22.

139 Ronald E. Powaski, *Return to Armageddon: The United States and the Nuclear Arms Race, 1981–1999* (New York: Oxford University Press, 2000), 226.

140 *Washington Post*, 19 May 2002, 9.

141 Walter Lippmann, *Public Opinion* (New Brunswick, N.J.: Transaction Publishers, 1997), 386.

142 *New York Times*, 21 September 1998, 1.

143 Peter Grose, *Gentleman Spy: The Life of Allen Dulles* (Boston: Houghton Mifflin, 1994), 292.

144 *Washington Post*, 9 September 2002, 17.

145 In its short history, NIMA has been responsible for a series of major intelligence disasters, including the failure to monitor Indian nuclear testing in 1998, the bombing of the Chinese embassy in Belgrade in 1999, and the exaggeration of missile programs in North Korea and Iran.

CULTURE

146 Carl Weiser, "Bush Administration Struggles to Build U.S. 'Brand' Abroad," Gannett News Service, 10 July 2002.

147 "What is Operation TIPS?" *Washington Post*, 14 July 2002.

148 Ellen Sorokin, "Security Bill Loses ID Card, TIPS," *Washington Times*, 19 July 2002.

149 Joseph Nye, "Why Military Power Is No Longer Enough," *Observer Worldview*, 31 March 2001.

150 Colin Powell, from remarks at NetDiplomacy 2001 Conference, Washington, D.C., 6 September 2001.

151 Marc Cooper, "Lights! Cameras! Attack! Hollywood Enlists," *The Nation*, 10 December 2001.

152 Jane Perlez, "Muslim-as-Apple-Pie Videos Are Greeted With Skepticism," *New York Times*, 30 October 2002.

153 Katherine Seelye, "TV Drama, Pentagon-Style: A Fictional Terror Tribunal," *New York Times*, 31 March 2002.

154 Marion McKeone, "New York's Catharsis Begins; With a Month to the Anniversary of 11 September, New York Artists and Writers Are Scrambling to Convey a Changed New York Society," *Sunday Tribune*, 11 August 2002, 2.

155 Maureen Dowd, "Coyote Rummy," *New York Times*, 24 February 2002, Section 4, 13.

156 Elizabeth Becker, "A Nation Challenged: Hearts and MindsA Special Report; In the War on Terrorism, a Battle to Shape Opinion," *New York Times*, 11 November 2001, Section 1A, 1.

157 *NewsHour with Jim Lehrer*, "Limits of Dissent," 16 October 2001.

158 Bill Maher, *Politically Incorrect*, 17 September 2001.

159 Ari Fleischer, press briefing, 26 September 2001.

160 Peter Marks, "An Iconoclast's Last Days on His Late-Night Soapbox," *New York Times*, 23 June 2002, Section 2, 25.

161 James Dao and Eric Schmitt, "Pentagon Readies Efforts to Sway Sentiment Abroad," *New York Times*, 19 February 2002.

162 Donald Rumsfeld, Defense Department news briefing, 26 February 2002.

163 Howard Kurtz, "Journalists Worry About Limits on Information, Access," *Washington Post*, 24 September 2001, Section A, 5.

164 Elizabeth Becker, 1.

165 Carl Weiser, "PR campaign stretches from Iowa to Egypt," Gannett News Service, July 17, 2002.

166 Karen DeYoung, "Bush to Create Formal Office to Shape U.S. Image Abroad," *Washington Post*, 30 July 2002, Section A, 1.

167 Samer Shehata, "Why Bush's Middle East Propaganda Campaign Won't Work," Salon.com, 12 July 2002.

168 Paul Ackerman, et al. "Public Diplomacy: A Strategy for Reform, A Report of an Independent Task Force on Public Diplomacy Sponsored by the Council on Foreign Relations," Council on Foreign Relations, July 2002.

169 Ibid.

170 Ibid.

171 Jon Frandsen, "U.S. Seen as Global Big Kid with an Attitude," Gannett News Service, 11 July 2002.

CENTRAL ASIA

172 On August 26, 2002, Secretary of State Colin Powell testified to Congress that Uzbekistan had made substantial progress in improving human rights conditions in the country. He made the statement in order to allow Congress to ratify another $45 million in aid.

MIDDLE EAST

173 "Bush's Support for Reformers Backfires in Iran," *Washington Post*, 3 August 2002, A12.

174 Ibid.

175 Paul Rogers, "The Coming War with Iraq," *Open Democracy*, 20 February 2002.

176 U.S. Department of State, *Patterns of Global Terrorism—2001* (Washington, D.C.: Government Printing Office, 2002).

177 Sameer Yacoub, "Ex-Arms Inspector Says Attack on Iraq 'Not Justified,'" *Washington Post*, 9 September 2002.

178 Jim Lobe, "Hawks Control U.S. Middle East Policy," *Alternet*, 2 April 2002.

179 For example, Feith—prior to joining the administration—contributed to a 1996 paper that advised Israeli Prime Minister Netanyahu to make "a clean break from the peace process." See, e.g., "A Clean Break: A New Strategy for Securing the Realm," Institute for Advanced Strategic and Political Studies, June 1996, with Richard Perle as principal author. Similarly, Feith wrote a widely read 1997 article that called on Israel to reoccupy "the areas under Palestinian Authority control" even though "the price in blood would be high." Douglas Feith, "A Strategy for Israel," *Commentary*, September 1997.

180 Alan Sipress, "Policy Divide Thwarts Powell in Mideast Effort," *Washington Post*, 26 April 2002.

181 Office of the Press Secretary, "President Bush Calls for New Palestinian Leadership," press release (Washington, D.C., 24 June 2002).

182 Ibid.

AFRICA

183 "Maasai's 'Ultimate Gift' of Cows to US," *The Nation* (Nairobi), 4 June 2002.

184 Kevin Kelley, "No Cash for African Bomb Victims," *The Nation* (Nairobi), 22 May 2002.

185 "Ethiopia, US Coordinate Efforts Against Terrorism," Xinhua General News Agency, 10 December 2002; "Caution in Eritrea" (editorial), *Boston Globe*, 12 December 2002.

186 Charlie Cobb Jr., "Sub-Saharan Africa Rallies to US Support," allAfrica.com, 18 September 2002, available at allafrica.com/stories/20010919421.html; Office of the Coordinator for Counterterrorism, U.S. Department of State, "Africa Overview," in *Patterns of Global Terrorism—2001*, (Washington, D.C.: Government Printing Office, 21 May 2002), available at www.state.gov/s/ct/rls/pgtrpt/2001/ html/10236.htm.

187 Stephen Morrison, "Somalia's and Sudan's Race to the Fore in Africa," *The Washington Quarterly*, Spring 2002; Basildon Peta, "Viewpoint: Defying Mugabe's Crackdown," BBC News, 1 February 2001, available at news.bbc.co.uk/1/hi/world/africa/1750004.stm.

188 See a comparison of figures at www.adherents.com/Na_321.html.

189 Danna Harman, "US War on Terrorism Quietly Enters Phase 2," *Christian Science Monitor*, 2 January 2002; Ted Dagne, "Africa and the War on Terrorism," Congressional Research Service, 17 January 2002.

190 Harman, "US War on Terrorism."

191 U.S. Department of State, "Africa Overview."

192 Dena Montague, "Is Peace Possible Under NEPAD," Arms Trade Resource Center, 24 July 2002.

193 "UN Officials Say US Eyes New Terrorism Front," *Financial Times*, 12 December 2001; Kevin Kelly, "U.S. Seeks Proxy Froces in War against Terror," allAfrica.com, 10 January 10 2002, available at www.allafrica.com/stories/200201100630.html.

194 "Mubarak on International Terrorism," excerpt from CNN interview, 18 September 2001, available at www.sis.gov.eg/terrorism/html/ et39.htm.

195 Quoted in Réda Bensmaïa, "Reactions of Maghrebi People and States to the Attacks of September 11th," (Providence, RI: Watson Center, Brown University, 24 October 2001).

196 allAfrica.com, "Focus on Terrorism, and the Challenge for the AU," 23 July 2002, available at allafrica.com/stories/200207240007.html.

197 Peter Bergen, *Holy War, Inc* (New York: The Free Press, 2001), 22.

198 Vernon Loeb, "U.S. Considers Array of Actions Against Bin Laden," *Washington Post*, 3 December 2000.

199 Ed Warner, "Sudan and Terrorism," *Voice of America News Report*, 10 July 2002.

200 *MBR: Southern Africa Monthly Regional Bulletin* 10/09 (September 2001), available at southscan.gn.apc.org/samples/mrb0901_copy.html. If you take the 11th of September as the beginning of the new world order, [Sudanese officials] signaled they want to be on the right side," said one U.S. official. "They're opening the files, and, in a couple of cases, they've given us more than we asked for." Quoted in Jim Lobe, "U.S.-Sudan Terrorism Ties Spell Disaster for Anti-Khartoum Activists," Self-determination News, *Foreign Policy in Focus*, (Silver City, NM & Washington, DC: Foreign Policy in Focus, 25 September 2001).

201 Mbendi Information, "Sudan: Oil And Gas Industry," 16 August 2001, available at www.mbendi.co.za/indy/oilg/af/su/p0005.htm.

202 Andrew Borowie, "Maghreb Sees War as Vindication," *Washington Times*, 18 October 2001.

203 Sally Weymouth, "The Former Face of Evil," *Newsweek*, 20 January 2003; Todd Zeranski, "Bush Extends 17-Year-Old Economic Sanctions on Libya," *Bloomberg News*, 6 January 2003; Lucy Adams, "Britain and US in Rift over Libyan Lockerbie Apology," Sunday *Times* (London), 1 December 2002.

204 Scott Anderson, "The Makeover," *The New York Times Magazine*, 19 January 2003, 66.

205 U.S. Department of State, *Patterns of Global Terrorism—2001*.

206 Dennis O'Brien, "Norfolk Ship Has Goal to Defeat Al-Qaida," *Virginian-Pilot* (Norfolk), 5 January 2003.

207 The United States was negotiating, as well, with both Ethiopia and Eritrea about creating additional bases there. Paul Magnusson, "An American Outpost in

Africa," *Business Week*, 13 January 2003; Neal Conan, "Talk of the Nation," National Public Radio, 18 November 2002.

208 "Kenya Offers Cash Reward for Info on Bombing Suspects," *Israel Faxx*, 9 December 2002; "Arab TV: Al-Qaeda Claims Responsibility for Kenya Attack," *Israel Faxx*, 9 December 2002.

209 Rob Taylor, "Fed: Australia Changes Travel Warnings for Zanzibar," *AAP Newsfeed*, January 16, 2003; Richard Beeston, "Delayed Alert in Zanzibar put Tourists at Risk," *The Times* (London), January 16, 2003.

210 James Dao, "In Quietly Courting Africa, White House Likes Dowry," *New York Times*, 19 September 2002, 1-A.

211 Dena Montague, "Africa: The New Oil and Military Frontier," Arms Trade Resource Center Update, 20 September 2002.

212 National Intelligence Council, "Global Trends 2015," December 2000, available at www.cia.gov/cia/publications/globaltrends2015/.

213 National Energy Policy Development Group, Washington, D.C., May 2001.

214 James Dao, "In Quietly Courting Africa, White House Likes Dowry," *New York Times*, 19 September 2002, A1,6.

215 Ibid.

216 Ibid.

217 Montague, "Africa: The New Oil and Military Frontier."

218 Lora Lumpe, "U.S. Foreign Military Training," (Silver City, NM & Washington, DC: Foreign Policy in Focus, May 2002, 8.

219 Ibid., 14.

220 Ted Dagne, "Africa and the War on Terrorism," Congressional Research Service, 17 January 2002.

221 Kevin Kelley, "Moi's Farewell Trip to US," *The East African*, 9 December 2002.

222 Emily Wax, "Opposition Ends Decades of One-Party Rule in Kenya," *Washington Post*, 30 December 2002; "Heckled Moi Congratulates Kibaki," Agence France Presse, 30 December 2002.

223 Quoted in in Ken Silvestein, "Comrades in Arms," *Washington Monthly*, January/February 2002.

224 "US to Build Logistics Depot in Sierra Leone," *Concord Times* (Freetown), 26 July 2002, available at allafrica.com/stories/200207260244.html.

225 Ted Dagne, "Africa and the War on Terrorism," Congressional Research Service, 17 January 2002, 4.

226 Egyptian State Information Service, "Excerpts from President Hosni Mubarak's [Interview] to *Le Figaro*," 22 September 2001, available at www.sis.gov.ed/online/html4/o290921t.htm.

227 Salih Booker, "AIDS: Another World War," *The Nation*, 7 January 2002.

228 U.S. Africa policy, set out in the administration of George Bush Sr. in the early 1990s, states that "U.S. security policy and military programs should comple-

ment popular democratic reform and maintain adequate contact and influence with African military counterparts."(*National Security Review* 30: "American Policy Toward Africa in the 1990s" *ACAS Bulletin*, Winter 1993. Since the early days of the Cold War, "national security" has been the underlying theme of U.S. foreign policy; it was given a new and dramatic thrust by the attacks of September 11.

229 U.S. Department of Commerce, Bureau of Economic Analysis, "U.S. Direct Investment Abroad: Capital Flows—Annual and Quarterly Tables," updated 26 September 2002, available at www.bea.doc.gov/bea/di/di1usdbud.htm.

230 Caitlin Harrington, "Africa Needs More Aid to Combat Terrorism, Lawmakers Say," *Congressional Quarterly Daily Monitor*, 10 December 2002.

231 "Nelson Mandela: The U.S.A. is a Threat to World Peace," *Newsweek*, September 10, 2002; Gary Younge, "No More Mr. Nice Guy," *The Guardian* (London), September 19, 2002.

LATIN AMERICA

232 Letter to President George Bush by House International Relations Committee Chairman Henry Hyde, 27 October 2002, in which he refers to Cuba, Brazil, and Venezuela as a potential "axis of evil" in the Americas.

233 U.S. Department of State, *Patterns of Global Terrorism—2001*, (Washington, D.C.: Government Printing Office, 21 May 2002), 48.

234 Nancy Dunne and James Wilson, "Colombian Rebels Indicted," *Financial Times*, 19 March 2002.

235 Michael Shifter, "A Shaken Agenda: Bush and Latin America," *Current History*, February 2002, 55.

236 Jason Hagen, interview by the author, 16 July 2002.

237 William E. Gibson, "Plea for More Military Aid to Colombia Met with Doubt," *Fort Lauderdale Sun-Sentinel*, 12 April 2002.

238 Michael T. Klare, "Global Petro-Politics: The Foreign Policy Implications of the Bush Administration's Energy Plan," *Current History*, March 2002, 104.

239 David Corn, "Our Gang in Venezuela?" *The Nation*, 5/12 August 2002, 27.

240 Ibid., 26.

241 Rachel Farley, interview by the author, 13 August 2002.

242 Judith Miller, "Washington Accuses Cuba of Germ-Warfare Research," *New York Times*, 7 May 2002.

243 Audrey Hudson, "Officials Insist Carter Not Briefed on Cuban Arms," *Washington Times*, 15 May 2002.

244 Harold Olmos, "U.S.: Colombia Needs Free Trade," Associated Press, 9 July 2002.

245 See the State Department's list at www.state.gov/s/ct/rls/fs/2002/12389.htm.

246 U.S. Department of State, *Patterns of Global Terrorism—2001*, 45–46.

247 Testimony before the Senate Judiciary Subcommittee on Technology, Terrorism, and Government Information, 13 March 2002.

248 Adam Isacson, "Colombia Peace in Tatters," *NACLA Report on the Americas* XXXV(5) (March/April 2002): 11.

249 Steven Dudley, "War in Colombia's Oilfields," *The Nation*, 5/12 August 2002, 31.

250 Isacson, 12–13.

251 Joseph Contreras, "A 'Little Vietnam'?" *Newsweek International*, 15 June 2002.

ASIA

252 During the Gulf War, Japan contributed minesweepers and about $10.8 billion out of the estimated $60 billion it cost to fight the war, but those only after the hostilities had ended. See Yukio Okamoto, "Japan and the United States: The Essential Alliance," *Washington Quarterly* 25(20) (Spring 2002): 59–72.

253 The report was published in late 2000 by the Institute for National Strategic Studies under the title "The United States and Japan: Advancing Toward a Mature Partnership," and is available online at http://www.ndu.edu/ndu/ sr_japan.html. In addition to Armitage, key Bush administration officials who participated in drafting the report include: Paul Wolfowitz (deputy undersecretary of defense), James Kelly (assistant secretary of state for East Asia and the Pacific), and Torkel Patterson (former senior director for Asian affairs, National Security Council).

254 Japanese Prime Minister Junichiro Koizumi has called for the repeal, or at least a reinterpretation of, Article 9 of Japan's constitution, which forbids Japan to wage war. A reinterpretation would allow Japan to use military force as part of "collective security" operations; that is, to assist allied forces under attack outside of Japanese territory.

255 For the June 2001 policy review, see "Statement by the President," 13 June 2001, available at www.whitehouse.gov/news/releases/2001/06/20010611-4.html. For Bush's March 2001 comments, see "Remarks by President Bush and President Kim Dae-Jung of South Korea," 7 March 2001, available at www.white-house.gov/news/releases/2001/03/20010307-6.html. For Powell's remarks, see "Press Availability with Her Excellency Anna Lindh, Minister of Foreign Affairs of Sweden," 6 March 2001, available at www.state.gov/secretary/ rm/2001/1116.htm.

256 See their comments at Agence France-Presse ("US Slams 'Evil' North Korea's Weapons Proliferation," 29 August 2002), where Bolton denounced the DPRK as "an evil regime that is armed to the teeth including with weapons of mass destruction and ballistic missiles."

257 International Crisis Group, "Indonesian-U.S. Military Ties," 17 July 2001, 7, available at www.crisisweb.org/projects/asia/indonesia/reports/ A400360_18072001.pdf.

258 See John Gershman, "Is Southeast Asia the Second Front?" *Foreign Affairs*, July/August 2002, 60–74; International Crisis Group, "Al-Qaeda in Southeast Asia: The Case of the "Ngruki Network" in Indonesia," 8 August 2002, available at www.crisisweb.org/ projects/asia/indonesia/reports/A400733_08082002.pdf; and "Indonesia Backgrounder: How The Jemaah Islamiyah Terrorist Network Operates," January 2003, available at www.crisisweb.org/projects/asia/indonesia/reports/A400845_11122002.pdf.

259 See collection of newspaper articles on the guidance at www.yale.edu/strattech/92dpg.html. For a discussion of the debate with respect to China, see Thomas J. Christensen, "Posing Problems without Catching Up: China's Rise and Challenges for U.S. Security Policy," *International Security* 25(4) (Spring 2001): 5–40.

260 For a useful discussion see David Shambaugh, "Sino-American Strategic Relations: From Partners to Competitors," *Survival* 42(1) (Spring 2000): 97–115.

261 See Jim Lobe and Tom Barry, "Yellow Peril Revisited," 12 July 2002 available at www.fpif.org/commentary/2002/0207china.html; and Lawrence F. Kaplan, "United Nations: China's War on Terrorism and Ours," *New Republic*, 22 July 2002, 20–24.

262 See www.uscc.gov and www.defenselink.mil/news/Jul2002/d20020712china.pdf.

263 For an article that makes a similar argument, see David Shambaugh, "Sino-American Relations since September 11: Can the New Stability Last?" *Current History*, September 2002.

RESPONSE

264 Jean-Marie Colombani, "We Are All Americans," *Le Monde*, 12 September 2001.

265 A majority of Europeans, for instance, believe that U.S. foreign policy was in part responsible for the September 11 attacks. See polls in Worldviews 2, available at 208.141.197.179/key_findings/transatlantic_report.htm#kf1.

266 "Nations Around World Condemn Terror Attacks on U.S.," Reuters, 12 September 2001.

267 Louis Golino, "NATO Seen Adapting to Terror War; Alliance Used Only Sparingly after Attacks," *Washington Times*, 18 August 2002.

268 Edward Alden, "Europe Freezes Terrorist Assets Worth $35 Million," *Financial Times*, 7 April 2002.

269 Michael Baun, "EU Enlargement and Transatlantic Relations after September 11," American Institute for Transatlantic Studies, available at www.aicgs.org/eu/baun.shtml.

270 See discussion in Benjamin Schwarz and Christopher Layne, "A New Grand Strategy," *The Atlantic Monthly*, January 2002.

271 Jonathan Freedland, "Fury at President's 'Axis of Evil' Speech," *Guardian* (London), 9 February 2002.

272 Zdzislaw Lachowski, "The Military Dimension of the European Union," in *SIPRI Yearbook 2002* (Stockholm International Peace Research Institute, 2002).

273 Lawrence Kaplan, "France 1, America 0," *The New Republic*, 14 November 2000. Belgian foreign minister Louis Michel, meanwhile, criticized Blair for "grandstanding and warmongering" and declared that Europe "will not follow Bush and Blair blindfold." See also Martin Walker, "Post 9/11: The European Dimension," *World Policy Journal*, Winter 2001/02. For more on Europe's military options, see John Lloyd, "A Subaltern or a General?" *The New Statesman*, 22 July 2002.

274 "Who Needs Whom," *The Economist*, 9 March 2002, 32.

275 See, e.g., Lester Thurow, *Head to Head* (New York: William Morrow, 1992).

276 As such, the Bush administration is pushing for "a new international division of labor in which America does the bombing and fighting, the French, British, and German serve as police in the border zones, and the Dutch, Swiss, and Scandinavians provide humanitarian aid." Michael Ignatieff, "Barbarians at the Gate?" *The New York Review of Books*, 28 February 2002, 4.

277 See the EU's Web site for a summary of EU-Iran relations, europa.eu.int/comm/external_relations/iran/intro/.

278 Andrew Cottey, "September 11th 2001 One Year On: A New Era in World Politics? (Washington, D.C.: BASIC, September 2002), available at www.basicint.org/terrorism/cottey.htm.

279 Sam Dillon with Donald G. McNeil Jr., "Spain Sets Hurdles for Extraditions," *New York Times*, 24 November 2001.

280 Audrey Gillan, "Extradition to US of al-Qaida Suspect Fails," *Guardian* (London), July 22, 2002. There is evidence, however, that the EU may waive certain extradition requirements in a secret agreement with the United States. Richard Norton-Taylor, "Europe-US Terror Treaty Plan Raises Rights Fears," *Guardian* (London), 3 September 2002.

281 Geert Groot Koerkamp, "Moscow's Ties with Baghdad," *Radio Netherland*, 30 November 2001.

282 Quoted in *Newsweek*, 27 May 2002.

283 "Gates of Hell Will Open If US Attacks Iraq, Say Arab States," *Times* (London), 6 September 2002.

284 "Transcript of Press Conference by Secretary-General Kofi Annan at Headquarters," 19 December 2001, available at www.un.org/News/Press/docs/2001/sgsm8081.doc.htm.

285 See Raymond Colitt, "Serious Ideas Behind the Theatrics," *Financial Times*, 4 February 2002.

HOW THINGS SHOULD CHANGE

286 An August 15, 2002, press release by Friends of the Earth, "How to Sabotage a Summit: The Hidden hand of Exxon Revealed," quotes the August 2, 2002, letter. "We applaud the decision not to attend the Summit in person…," available at www.foei.org/media/2002/0815earth.htm.

287 With only 4 percent of the world's population, the United States consumes one-third of the world's natural resources. See Pamela Sparr, "Living Simply," *Response*, December 2000.

288 Program on International Policy Attitudes, "Americans on Foreign Aid and World Hunger: A Study of U.S. Public Attitudes," 2 February 2001, available at www.pipa.org/OnlineReports/BFW/conclusion.html.

289 U.S. Department of State, "Measure Suggests Using Foreign Aid as Anti-terrorism Tool," 5 February 2002, available at usinfo.state.gov/topical/pol/terror/02020606.htm.

290 Forty percent of the electorate, as the war wound down in early spring 2002, rejected the idea of an expanded war on terrorism. See Walter Shapiro, "Anti-anti-war Crowd Dreams Up a Disloyal Opposition," *USA Today*, 13 March 2002.

291 George Will, echoing other unilateralists, would like to see the UN go the way of the League of Nations. See "Stuck to the UN Tar Baby," *Washington Post*, 19 September 2002.

AFTERWORD

292 At the time, Secretary of State Madeleine Albright and other senior officials justified the self-defense label with reference to Article 51 of the UN Convention.

293 Senator John McCain (R-AZ) on August 20, 1998, said, "Today's military action against Osama bin Laden's terrorist infrastructure in Afghanistan and Sudan is a welcome response to the August 7 terrorist attacks against the American embassies in Kenya and Tanzania. I know I speak for all Americans in supporting the U.S. service members who took part in this operation, and in hoping that the strikes clearly signal our will to retaliate against terrorists who target American citizens abroad." As reported on the Federation of American Scientists Web site, www.fas.org/man/dod-101/ops/docs/98082802_ppo.html.

294 Secretary of State Madeleine Albright, from an interview on CNN's *Larry King Live*, 20 August 1998. As reported on the Federation of American Scientists Web site, www.fas.org/man/dod-101/ops/docs/98082101_tpo.html.

295 Analyses by Seymour Hersh, James Risen, and other journalists and scholars point out that there was considerable dissension in the Clinton administration over the bombings. Many questions remain about whether the Sudanese plant produced chemical weapons, which was the rationale for the attack. See Seymour M. Hersh, "The Missiles of August," *The New Yorker*, 12 October 1998, 34–41. Also see James Risen, "To Bomb Sudan Plant, or Not: A Year Later, Debates Rankle," *New York Times*, 27 October 1999.

296 Military responses to terrorist acts have been rare over the last few decades. Michelle Malvesti makes the interesting point that when this has occurred previously (i.e., bombings in Libya, Iraq, and Sudan/Afghanistan) the characteristics shared by the precipitating event included a direct hit on U.S. government interests rather than on private citizens. See Michele L. Malvesti, "Explaining the United States' Decision to Strike Back at Terrorists," *Terrorism and Political Violence* 13(2) (2001): 85–106.

297 The casualties from the Nairobi bombing were so extensive and severe in part because the U.S. embassy sorely needed security upgrades. The U.S. ambassador to Kenya at the time had asked for attention to security matters for months including just before the bombings.

298 Amber Amundson, "A Widow's Plea for Non-Violence," *Chicago Tribune*, 25 September 2001.

299 The U.S. NGO Global Exchange is campaigning for ten thousand dollars each to be given to approximately three thousand families. A congressional resolution, sponsored by Representatives Carrie Meek (D-FL) and John Cooksey (R-LA), has received the support of two dozen members.

300 See the Daniel Pearl Foundation home page, www.danielpearlfoundation.org/about_us/index.html.

301 Address by Mwalimu Julius K. Nyerere, Chairman of the South Centre, Gandhi Peace Prize Ceremony, New Delhi, India, 27 January 1996.

About the Contributors

TOM BARRY is a senior analyst at the Interhemispheric Resource Center (IRC), codirector of Foreign Policy in Focus (FPIF), and author of numerous books, including *Zapata's Revenge: Free Trade and Farm Crisis in Mexico* (South End, 1995).

BARBARA EHRENREICH is the author of numerous books, including *Blood Rites: On the Origins and History of the Passions of War* (Metropolitan Books, 1997) and *Nickeled and Dimed* (Metropolitan Books, 2001).

JOHN FEFFER is the author of *Shock Waves: Eastern Europe after the Revolutions* (South End, 1992), coeditor of *Europe's New Nationalism* (Oxford, 1996), and editor of *Living in Hope: People Challenging Globalization* (Zed, 2002).

JOHN GERSHMAN is a senior analyst at the IRC and Asia/Pacific editor for FPIF.

MELVIN A. GOODMAN is senior fellow at the Center for International Policy and coauthor of *The Wars of Eduard Shevardnadze* (Brassey, 2001) and *The Phantom Defense: America's Pursuit of the Star Wars Illusion* (Praeger, 2001).

WILLIAM D. HARTUNG is the director of the Arms Trade Resource Center, President's Fellow at the World Policy Institute, author of *And Weapons For All* (HarperCollins, 1994), and a member of FPIF's Advisory Committee.

SUSAN F. HIRSCH is associate professor of anthropology and women's studies at Wesleyan University in Middletown, Connecticut.

MARTHA HONEY is a fellow at the Institute for Policy Studies, codirector of the Peace and Security Program at the Institute for Policy Studies (IPS), and coeditor of *Global Focus: U.S. Foreign Policy at the Turn of the Millennium* (St. Martin's, 2000).

MICHAEL T. KLARE is a professor of peace and world security studies at Hampshire College in Amherst, Massachusetts, the author of *Resource Wars: The New Landscape of Global Conflict* (Metropolitan Books, 2001), and a member of FPIF's Advisory Committee.

ERIK LEAVER, who prepared the charts and graphs, is FPIF's congressional outreach coordinator.

JIM LOBE writes regularly for FPIF, Inter Press Service, OneWorld.net, and other publications and is a member of FPIF's Advisory Committee.

JULES LOBEL is a professor at the University of Pittsburgh Law School and vice president of the Center for Constitutional Rights.

MIRIAM PEMBERTON is a research fellow at IPS and Peace and Security Editor for FPIF.

AHMED RASHID is a journalist and author of the books *Taliban: Militant Islam and Fundamentalism in Central Asia* (Yale University, 2001) and *Jihad: The Rise of Militant Islam in Central Asia* (Yale University, 2001).

MICHAEL RATNER is president of the Center for Constitutional Rights and a professor at Columbia Law School.

NOY THRUPKAEW writes on culture for *The American Prospect.*

MARK WEISBROT is the codirector of the Center for Economic and Policy Research.

COLETTA YOUNGERS is senior associate at Washington Office on Latin America and a member of FPIF's Advisory Committee.

STEPHEN ZUNES is an associate professor of politics and chair of the Peace and Justice Studies Program at the University of San Francisco, Middle East Editor for FPIF, and author of *Tinderbox: U.S. Middle East Policy and the Roots of Terrorism* (Common Courage Press, 2002).

SPONSORING ORGANIZATIONS

FOREIGN POLICY IN FOCUS (FPIF), established in 1996, seeks to make the United States a more responsible global leader and global partner. It is a "think tank without walls" that functions as an international network of more than 650 policy analysts and advocates. Unlike traditional think tanks, FPIF is committed to advancing a citizen-based foreign policy agenda—one that is fundamentally rooted in citizen initiatives and movements.

FPIF is a collaborative project of the Interhemispheric Resource Center (IRC) and the Institute for Policy Studies (IPS).

THE INSTITUTE FOR POLICY STUDIES is the nation's oldest multi-issue progressive think tank. Since 1963, the Institute has worked with social movements to forge viable and sustainable policies to promote democracy, justice, human rights, and diversity. Based in Washington, DC, but with links to activists and scholars across the nation and around the world, the Institute serves as a bridge between progressive forces in government and grass-roots activists, and between movements in the U.S. and those in the developing world. We are proud to serve as an alternative voice, helping the least powerful to be heard in the halls of government and in the mainstream and independent press.

To facilitate long-term planning as well as rapid response to world events, IPS's projects are configured in three clusters, supported by an administrative and outreach cluster. Foreign Policy In Focus is grouped in the Peace and Security cluster along with projects on New Internationalism, Drug Policy, and Nuclear Policy. However, IPS seeks to foster interaction and collaboration among all staff so that our research cuts across academic disciplines to a broad view of how the world really works.

THE INTERHEMISPHERIC RESOURCE CENTER has been dedicated to working to make the United States a more responsible member of the global community since 1979. Through its two programs—Americas Program and Global Affairs Program—the IRC staff and board work to forge local-global links for policy alternatives, strategic dialogue, and citizen action.

To forward their objectives, the Global Affairs and Americas programs work with partners to develop strategic analysis in the form of policy briefs, special reports, talking points, commentaries, and similar materials. In addition to offering these materials online, by email, or via direct mailings, the IRC collaborates with dozens of advocacy and constituency groups to supply them with policy briefings and talking points for use in their own work on Capitol Hill or with their own constituencies.

The IRC also engages in issues of concern by taking part in events convened by other organizations as well as participating in collaborative organizing efforts such as the World Social Forum. In addition to global and regional work, the IRC maintains strong ties to the local community. In 2001, for instance, the IRC produced an in-depth report on the future of the copper mining industry in their hometown, Silver City, New Mexico.